C

JOBS
through the
INTERNET

[NEW GRADUATES]

Career Counsel
2002

Publised by
CAREER COUNSEL • LEICESTER
The Old Exchange, 449 Hinckley Road, Leicester, LE3 0WD, UK

A CIP catalogue record for this book is available from the British Library.

First Published 1998

Reprinted 1999

Second Edition 2000

Third Edition 2002

ISBN 1-902701-19-4

ADVERTISING SALES: 0116 223 2645

Printed in Great Britain by
Omnia Books, Glasgow, United Kingdom

Contents

Part One: Career Advice

Part Two: The Directory

Preface

Approximately 50% of all Graduate positions will be filled by Christmas. This is because most graduate recruiters begin their recruitment drive in September /October of the final year.

It is important therefore that, at the start of your final year you are armed with a list of who you would like to work for, their closing dates for applications, the locations and dates of their milkround visits and anything else you need to know in order to mount a well timed, professional, job hunting campaign.

Thankfully, the internet has made a wealth of information available to you and it is now easier and faster than ever to find and gather the information you need. It also allows you to plan your campaign during the holidays from the comfort of your own home.

This book is designed to help you.

Good luck!

The secret of their evolutionary success has been their ability to identify what they want, then work out a means of getting it

David Attenborough talking about the Bonobo Monkeys of Nothern Congo

Part One

Career Advice

Writing a C.V.

A well written and properly maintained c.v. will confirm your skills and experience to an employer, help get you an interview, prepare you to speak about yourself at interview and will help guide you toward those areas which you would like to develop further. There are three popular formats:

Reverse chronological is the simplest and most popular. Beginning with the most recent position it simply moves back through the applicant's career.

Functional c.v.'s focus on the applicants expertise, highlighting the skills they have developed and utilised in different roles. The style concentrates less on a chronological progression and more on outlining the applicants abilities, and is therefore ideal for contractors, consultants, and other careers where there may be gaps between jobs.

A **predictive** c.v. is used to create a favourable comparison between the individuals experience and a set of specific requirements. Candidates who are applying for one specific job will sometimes use a predictive c.v., as it allows them to tailor their own skills to those sought by the employer. Although effective, it is impractical to employ the predictive c.v. during a wide-ranging or potentially prolonged job hunt.

Most applicants should begin with the first format.

All c.v.'s will include information which falls into three broad categories: housekeeping, competencies (skills) and responsibilities. The following is a list of information relevant for all three formats.

Personal information: this should include your Christian name, surname, address, e-mail address and phone numbers. Include if at all possible a daytime one. If you are concerned about being contacted during the day then mark it to be used with discretion but try to leave it in.

Education: begin with your degree and work backwards. Details of which O levels or GCSE are unlikely to be important although if you have done an arts degree then it is worth stating that you also have Maths and likewise if you did science state your qualifications in English language.

Courses: briefly give the course name and where and when taken. Keep the details brief but ensure that what you learned is clear.

Languages: state those in which you have either written or oral fluency.

Memberships: state your current membership of relevant associations and trade bodies. Keep the list brief.

Interests: strike a balance between team and individual sports and intellectual and physical pastimes.

Work history: in a reverse chronological format this is the most important section, and can be used to communicate your competencies alongside your responsibilities and achievements. A functional or

Accomplished	Effected		Rectified
Achieved	Eliminated	Launched	Reinforced
Acquired	Empowered	Learned	Rendered
Activated	Encouraged	Led	Re-negotiated
Actively	Engineered	Listened	Renovated
Adjusted	Established		Reorganised
Administered	Estimated	Managed	Repaired
Analysed	Evaluated	Manipulated	Reported
Applied	Exceeded	Mechanised	Researched
Appraised	Expanded	Mediated	Responded
Approved	Expedited	Memorised	Responsible
Arranged		Merged	Revamped
Assembled	Facilitated	Modulated	Revised
Assisted	Finalised	Monitored	
Attained	Followed up	Motivated	Saved
Authorised	Forecast	Moulded	Scheduled
	Foresaw		Selected
Broadcast	Formulated	Negotiated	Solved
Budgeted	Fostered		Sorted
Built		Observed	Stimulated
Calculated	Generated	Operated	
Classified	Guarded	Organised	Streamlined
Coached	Guided	Oversaw	Strengthened
Communicated			Structured
Compiled	Headed	Participated	Succeeded
Completed	Helped	Perceived	Successfully
Conceived	Hired	Persuaded	Summarised
Conferred		Pinpointed	Supervised
Constructed	Implemented	Planned	
Co-ordinated	Improved	Prepared	Taught
Counselled	Increased	Presented	Tended
Created	Indexed	Presided	Trained
	Influenced	Produced	Transferred
Dealt with	Informed	Programmed	Transformed
Decided	Inspected	Projected	Translated
Defined	Installed	Proposed	Triggered
Delegated	Instituted		Trouble-shooting
Delivered	Instructed	Qualified	
Demonstrated	Interpreted	Queried	Uncovered
Designed	Introduced	Questioned	Utilised
Developed	Invented		
Directed	Investigated	Ran	Verified
		Recommended	Viewed
Edited	Judged	Reconciled	
			Went
			Wrote

Table 1: Use of action verbs enables you to offer both a more succinct and dynamic image.

predictive c.v. would offer a work history simply as a matter of record.

Responsibilities held: many can be incorporated into the work history but you may feel it worthwhile to highlight those of particular importance by listing them separately. Alternatively keep a separate list detailing those which you may have left out of the work history.

Achievements: these will establish your credibility and offer the employer some measure of the size of your responsibilities. Try to be specific.

Competencies (skills): many employers are now focussing entirely on these, particularly at a new graduate/first bouncer level and for technical roles. Be comprehensive, succinct and offer some measure or qualification. Transferable skills such as team playing, questioning, listening etc. may be better handled within work history or responsibilities.

In the last four categories you will find that the use of action verbs enables you to offer both a more succinct and dynamic image and those overleaf are suggested as a starting point. You will doubtless think of others.

Preparing Your Own C.V.

PETER BRUNSWICK
Career Consultant

The purpose of this article is to give you some help in improving your c.v. It is not an in depth guide to c.v. writing, offering instead a few practical ideas which you can apply today to your c.v. It is worth remembering that if you ask ten people how to lay out a c.v. you will get ten different answers. There is no such thing as a perfect layout. You will have to rely on your own judgement and whatever advice you find useful. Here's mine:

CONTENT:

Many c.v. writing guides place great store on the layout of a c.v., emphasising the need to keep to two pages and use particular titles and paper to gain advantage. In my opinion this is nonsense. Certainly the layout and style is important, but it is the content, above all which makes for a good c.v. Unless the content tells an employer that you can do the job then your application will get no further. Most of the content which goes into a c.v. falls into three areas:

1. Housekeeping

This includes your name, address, contact numbers (day and eve), e-mail, education, hobbies, marital status, children, current salary, relocation ability, driving license, other languages (unless required for the job).

By and large housekeeping is all the stuff that an employer will want to know about you but which is unlikely to form the main basis of their selection. Sure, they may need you to have a driving licence or the ability to relocate but all of the above are largely factual data, not open for interpretation. You've either got a driving licence or you haven't.

Some people think that current salary should be excluded and mentioned only in a covering letter. They may be right, but in my experience it is pointless missing it off. The first question the interviewer will ask is "What is your current salary?" and then they will write it onto your c.v. Before they make you an offer they need to have a clear idea of what will be necessary to attract you.

Date of birth, marital status and number of children is a more controversial subject. Speak to any careers advisor and they will tell you to leave it off. They may be right but be aware that whatever the law may say, employers are increasingly interested in knowing whether you will have to drop little Johnny off at nursery before travelling for an hour to work. If relocation is involved then they want to be sure that your partner is happy with your move and that they will support you in your decision. How you deal with these issues will say much about your commitment to your prospective employer and will impact on their decision. If you leave the information off they will simply write it on. My own advice has always been to be as open and honest as you can and to have a confidence about you bourne out of a realistic appraisal of your personal circumstances and how they will fit in with your prospective employer.

Employers rarely use any of this information in any case for selecting through c.v.'s in the first instance. An employer with 100 c.v.'s who does not want anyone over 45 would be wasting their time going through each one checking ages in a first pass to put to one side the three aged over 45. A glance at the more meaningful content of skills and responsibilities would enable them to eliminate sixty immediately. Only then will they look to check that the remaining forty each have a driving licence and are within their age paradigm and if your content is strong enough then they will shift their paradigm for you!

2. Responsibilities

A lot of people head this section 'Work Experience' or 'Career to Date'. The title is immaterial. Use any title you like. The content however *must encompass responsibilities*. Just consider for a moment what the employer is looking for. They are recruiting because they have a goal to achieve and they want someone to take *responsibility* for achieving it.

If for example they are trying to recruit a Production Line Manager in a fruit processing factory, they don't simply want someone who has had the title "Production Line Manager". They want someone who has taken responsibility for handling labour relations on the line, responsibility for ensuring quality control, responsibility for implementing new technology etc...

Many people are responsible for a lot more than they credit themselves with. Most of us attend meetings in our work. Think for a moment about your responsibilities in those meetings. If they are your meetings then it's fairly obvious: setting the agenda, scheduling the meeting, appointing a chairperson, timekeeper and someone to take the minutes. If, however, they are someone else's meetings then many people feel they have no responsibilities, which is of course wrong. They are responsible for turning up on time. For noting the meeting in their diary and reading the agenda beforehand. Within the meeting they are responsible for making a contribution themselves and helping others who are less confident to make their contribution. They are responsible for ensuring the meeting achieves its objectives without getting sidelined or splitting into secondary meetings.

Unless a candidate recognises their contribution to a meeting as an attendee then it is unlikely they will ever be promoted to managing the meeting itself. And unless they can communicate that knowledge by example or on a c.v. then they will not be considered for promotion.

One way of emphasising your responsibilities and of giving them credibility is to establish your position within the company:

'Reporting to the Managing Director I was responsible
for...'

'As Chief Engineer to the Firefly Project my
responsibilities were to...'

'As Head of Marketing for the Southern Region... '

Each of these three statements establishes that
applicants position within the organisation and adds
credibility to their claims.

Another way is to quantify your responsibilities. This
needs to be handled carefully, but used judiciously it allows
the employer to assess the credibility and size of your
responsibilities. Take for example the following:

'As Project Leader I was responsible for delivering a $
multi million section of the project on time.'

The generalisation of the costs implies duplicity and should
be avoided. Better would be:

'As Project Leader I was responsible for delivering a
$2.3 million section of the project on time.'

Being specific adds credibility.

Very often candidates have assumed responsibilities
which are not in their job spec. For example, within any
team there is always someone who is the recognised
technical guru or an expert on the order processing system.
Those responsibilities may not be spelt out in their job
definition but they none the less exist. And everyone
expects them to fulfil those responsibilities. They should
get it down on their c.v: "As the most experienced member
of the team my responsibilities included being the centre of
competence on the order processing system.'

For every responsibility which you have there will be
some associated action which you carried out to fulfil your
responsibility.

There is no harm in including some of your actions in your c.v. It gives some indication of your style and approach and will be welcomed by the reader. The same is true for your achievements. But remember, employers are looking for your responsibilities. Use your actions simply to demonstrate your confidence in fulfilling your responsibilities. Always think: Does it add value? Is it credible? The bulk of your actions will be handled at the interview. It is all too easy to end up writing a book on how you fulfilled your responsibilities. Employers will not want to read your book.

3. Skills

This is a list of what you can do set against some qualifying statement of how well you can do it. All jobs require some skills and as you progress through your career you should be looking to add to your skills base (and thus to your value). Again most candidates underestimate their skills.

For example a Pharmacist will need to know how to handle the computer systems which print out the labels to go on the prescriptions as they are dispensed. These tend to be standard systems which additionally handle stock reordering etc. Most pharmacists will have experience of a number of these systems but fail to regard it as a skill. And yet, when someone who has only ever used one system is asked to work on a different one, they are at a loss to do so. Likewise a Pharmacy Manager might be expected to buy one of these systems. If you were applying for the Pharmacy Manager's position, the ability to understand a number of different systems and the differences between them would add value to your application. State your skill and differentiate yourself from the competition.

There is increasing emphasis these days on transferable skills. These include good questioning and listening skills, meeting skills and interview skills. Many organisations spend vast sums training their employees in these skills and the individuals then fail to add them to their c.v.'s. This is a mistake. They take up very little space and add a lot of measurable value: 'Effective Communication – course attended July 1996.' Additionally it tells them that if they send you on a course their money won't be wasted.

Many candidates omit skills which they have because they don't want to use them. Again, this should be avoided. If you don't want to use a particular skill any more then don't apply for jobs involving it. Don't, for goodness sake, remove it from your list of skills. It shows that you can do it and have done it in the past. Quantify it by all means with a comment like when you last used it and how long you used it for. Show a scale of 1-5 that it is no longer your current strength. Emphasise in your covering letter that you do not wish to use that skill and would not accept an offer in that direction. But do not delete an important skill from your c.v. If the skill is a programming language for example then it demonstrates that you have an aptitude for languages, that you have good experience of structure and format. It shows that, were they to spend money training you in a different language, there is a good chance you will be a quick learner.

We recently handled the recruitment of the IT director for a major Corporation. The successful candidate had reached a level where he was unlikely to go near a computer and yet the skills section on his c.v. ran to 4 pages, all supported by some evidence and qualification. This told his prospective employers two things: firstly, no-one in the department was going to pull the wool over his eyes and secondly, that any recommendations which the individual made concerning changes to the IT system were likely to be the right ones for the business rather than those he was simply familiar with from previous experience. It also communicated at a glance that he had extensive experience and that his c.v. should be considered further.

The same holds true for all other skills.

LAYOUT AND STYLE:

There are two facts which govern the layouts of c.v.'s. The first is that your c.v. will be one of tens if not hundreds. The implication is that it will not be read in the first instance. Almost all employers or consultants will make three piles based on a *GLANCE* at the c.v: those that are YES, those that are NO and those that are MAYBE. It is vital therefore that your c.v. communicates effectively *AT A GLANCE.*

The second fact about c.v.'s is that the employer will then give all those in the YES pile to his secretary for copying. At this point all your fancy covers and expensive paper will count for nothing. The photo you stuck on the front will get lost in the copier and the secretary's efforts in undoing the binding which you fitted will result in a torn original. The only time a fancy, bound c.v. is relevant is when you know that you are one of only two or three being considered or if you provide an unbound extra copy for copying purposes. Otherwise *keep it simple.* Single sided A4 will do nicely.

There are a couple of tips which should be bourne in mind:

Be succinct. This does *not* mean keep it to two pages. This means putting in only that which adds value and saying what you want to say with a minimum of words. You will then find that you have plenty of space to include all your other responsibilities and skills.

Keep a Clear Layout. A logical layout would keep all the Housekeeping factual information together, followed by your Responsibilities in reverse chronological order, followed by a list of Skills. What headings and layout you chose is up to you. However the following should be noted:

Try to use bold text, capitals, underlines and indents both judiciously and consistently. It is my hope that you will find this article a good example of a clear layout.

Concentrate particularly on having consistent and logical headings. If you keep all the housekeeping on one page then the reader can just skim over that page using it only for reference. Many people split their housekeeping up so that they can get their skills onto the front page in the belief that it will create a more arresting c.v. My opinion is that the benefits of having all the housekeeping together for clarity outweigh the alleged disadvantages of having your best selling points under the front page.

Label and number each page. If they are going to break it up for copying then you need to make it as easy as possible to reassemble. Have your name and a page number on every page.

Keep to single sided A4. This makes copying easier and ensures that the copy will contain all of your c.v. and not just the even pages!

THINGS TO AVOID:

This is purely subjective but many of my clients take the same view as I do!

Unique Selling Propositions: The Unique Selling Proposition is a bit of sales jargon which has entered the recruitment world. It is true that if you have a unique skill such as a rare foreign language which the client requires then they will take you on. You should be aware of this and keep your eyes open for the opportunity. This is simply good sales practice. But it is also true that 99 time out of a 100 you will find that you are not unique, that there are twelve billion other souls like you. Or you will find that the employer does not want your USP, and does not want you to foist it on them. Employers simply want professional people who can handle the responsibility of the job. A considered, professional approach will beat a USP any day.

Candidate Profiles / Summaries: In my experience these tend to be woolly repetitions of the content of a c.v. They are often included because the author has not been succinct enough within the body of the c.v. No employer will put a c.v. into the YES pile on the basis of a summary. Many however will add it to the NO pile.

Photographs: Unless you are applying for a modelling or acting role then no one is employing you for your looks. A photograph carries the message that you are not confident about the c.v. standing out on its own merits. That it needs a pretty picture to help it along. The same applies to covers and fancy coloured paper.

Clichéd phrases such as 'Work well as part of a team and as an individual': This phrase is so clichéd that it should never be used. It is found on so many c.v.'s that someone must be lying! If you do work well in a team then you will have responsibilities towards your team. Put *them* on your c.v. Or you may have been on a team building course in which case it may be under your skills section. If you work well as an individual then you will have fulfilled your individual responsibilities and should say as much in the c.v. It is a woolly phrase, often found in summaries, which tells the reader that the rest of the c.v. is likely to lack **substance.**

Third Person statements such as "David is responsible for... etc…". This is *your* c.v., not somebody else's! At some point in the past candidates with these c.v.'s were told not to use the word *I*. They avoided it by using the third person. In my opinion this misses the point. You should not use the word I, or any other word for that matter unless it adds value to your c.v. There is little point in saying 'I am responsible for...' when 'Responsible for...' will suffice.

In short always remember what the employer is looking for: a professional person who can handle the responsibilities of the job. Keep it clear, succinct and precise and you will already be way ahead of the pack. If you find at the end that you are still dissatisfied with the c.v. then it is probably because, in your heart of hearts, you too recognise that it lacks substance. Do not despair. Read the CONTENT section again and consider what responsibilities and skills you have and have had that you have failed to recognise. They are there, believe me!

PETER BRUNSWICK *is a freelance career consultant. He is author of The Recruitment Paradigm: How to move it to your advantage.*

Succinct Writing
STEPHEN BROUGH
The Economist Books

When presenting yourself in a c.v. and any accompanying correspondence, the way in which you write and use words is crucial. Sloppy or cumbersome writing indicates a sloppy or cumbersome brain at work. Here is some advice from the style guide used by those who write for *The Economist,* the world's most authoritative business and current affairs magazine, which is admired as much for the quality of its writing as it is for the quality of its analysis.

'Clarity of writing usually follows clarity of thought. So think what you want to say, then say it as simply as possible. Keep in mind George Orwell's six elementary rules ("Politics and the English Language", 1946):

1. Never use a METAPHOR, simile or other figure of speech which you are used to seeing in print.
2. Never use a long word where a SHORT WORD will do.
3. If it is possible to cut out a word, always cut it out.
4. Never use the passive where you can use the ACTIVE.
5. Never use a FOREIGN PHRASE, a scientific word or a JARGON word if you can think of an everyday English equivalent.
6. Break any of these rules sooner than say anything outright barbarous.

Readers are primarily interested in what you have to say. By the way in which you say it you may encourage them either to read on or to stop reading. If you want them to read on:

1. Do not be stuffy. "To write a genuine, familiar or truly English style", said Hazlitt, "is to write as anyone would speak in common conversation who had a thorough command or choice of words or who could discourse with ease, force and perspicuity setting aside all pedantic and oratorical flourishes."

   Use the language of everyday speech, not that of spokesmen, lawyers or bureaucrats (so prefer **let** to **permit**, **people** to **persons**, **buy** to **purchase**,

colleague to **peer**, **way out** to **exit**, **present** to **gift**, **rich** to **wealthy**, **break** to **violate**).

2. Do not be hectoring or arrogant. Those who disagree with you are not necessarily stupid or insane. Nobody needs to be described as silly: let your analysis prove that he is. When you express opinions, do not simply make assertions. The aim is not just to tell readers what you think, but to persuade them; if you use arguments, reasoning and evidence, you may succeed. Go easy on the oughts and shoulds.

3. Do not be too pleased with yourself. Don't boast of your own cleverness by telling readers that you correctly predicted something or that you have a scoop. You are more likely to bore or irritate them than to impress them.

4. Do not be too chatty. **Surprise, surprise** is more irritating than informative. So is **Ho, ho,** etc.

5. Do not be too didactic. If too many sentences being **Compare, Consider, Expect, Imagine, Look at, Note, Prepare for , Remember,** or **Take,** readers will think they are reading a textbook.

6. Do not be sloppy in the construction of your sentences and paragraphs. Do not use a participle unless you make it clear what it applies to. Thus avoid **Having died, they had to bury him,** or **Proceeding along this line of thought, the cause of the train crash becomes clear.**

Don't overdo the use of **don't, isn't, can't, won't,** etc. In general, be concise. Try to be economical in your account or argument ("the best way to be boring is to leave nothing out" – Voltaire). Similarly, try to be economical with words.

Do your best to be lucid. Simple sentences help. Keep complicated constructions and gimmicks to a minimum, if necessary by remembering the *New Yorker's* comment: "Backward ran sentences until reeled the mind". Mark Twain described how a good writer treats sentences: "At times he may indulge himself with a long one, but he will make sure there are no folds in it, no vagueness, no parenthetical interruptions of its view as a whole; when he has done with it, it won't be a sea-serpent with half of its arches under the water; it will be a torch-light procession."

Long paragraphs, like long sentences, can confuse the reader. "The paragraph," according to Fowler, "is essentially a unit of thought, not of length; it must be homogeneous in subject matter and sequential in treatment." One-sentence paragraphs should be used only occasionally.

Remember that some words add nothing but length to your prose. Use adjectives to make your meaning more precise and be cautious of those you find yourself using to make it more emphatic. The word **very** is a case in point. If it occurs in a sentence you have written, try leaving it out. **The omens were good** may have more force than **The omens were very good.**

Shoot off, or rather shoot, as many prepositions after verbs as possible. Thus people can **meet** rather than **meet with**; companies can be **bought** and **sold** rather than **bought up** and **sold off;** budgets can be **cut** rather than **cut back;** plots can be **hatched** but not **hatched up;** organisations should be **headed** rather than **headed up** by chairmen, just as markets should be **freed** rather than **freed up.** And children can be **sent** to bed rather than **sent off** to bed.

Use words with care. A **heart condition** is usually a **bad heart. Positive thoughts** presumably means **optimism,** just as a **negative report** is probably a **critical report. Industrial action** is usually **industrial inaction, industrial disruption** or **strike.** A **substantially finished** bridge is an **unfinished** bridge, a **major speech** usually just a **speech.** Something with **reliability problems** probably **does not work.** If yours is a **live audience,** what would a dead one be like?

Use short words where you can. They are easy to spell and easy to understand. Thus prefer **about** to **approximately, after** to **following, let** to **permit, but** to **however, use** to **utilise, make** to **manufacture, plant** to **facility, take part** to **participate, set up** to **establish, enough** to **sufficient, show** to **demonstrate,** and so on. **Under-developed** countries are often better described as **poor. Substantive** usually means **real** or **big.**

Clear thinking is the key to clear writing. "A scrupulous writer," observed Orwell, "in every sentence that he writes will ask himself at least four questions, thus: What am I trying to say? What words will express it? What image or idiom will make it clearer? Is this image fresh enough to have an effect? And he will probably ask himself two more: Could I put it more shortly? Have I said anything that is avoidably ugly?'

STEPHEN BROUGH *is the Editorial Director of Profile Books, publishers of The Economist Style Guide, and other Economist Books.*

Consider the Numbers

PETER BRUNSWICK

Career Consultant

In the US every advertised job attracts, on average, over 100 respondents. That must mean that each person seeking a job is sending out 100 enquiries before they are successful. This is an horrific thought. To get 100 copies of your c.v. out in response to 100 adverts is an awful lot of work. The good news is that both you, and I, know that you are not your average person! Historically you have found that, as a professional person, you have applied for fewer than ten positions before being made an offer. It follows therefore that to make up the numbers there must be some sad individual out there who has sent off thousands of applications and had no luck. And we keep seeing them on TV. Whenever unemployment is in the news they pull this hapless individual in front of the cameras and we listen to their sad tale, that despite having good qualifications they have had no response to over 1000 applications.

There are two lessons to be drawn from this.

The first is that, even as a professional, you will have to apply to nearly twenty positions in order to be offered just two, and thereby give yourself a choice.

The second is that if you don't do it right then it is possible to send out all the applications in the world and get no response.

It is essential therefore that to maximise your choice of jobs you find a way of approaching sufficient employers in an effective manner.

These numbers are based on averages and will vary from individual to individual and from industry to industry.

But the fact is that if you really want to get another job then sending off one or two applications is unlikely to deliver. I have been in recruitment for over fifteen years and even my ratio of candidates on final interviews to offers has rarely dipped below 5:1. And that is a pretty respectable effort! So if you want to have a choice of two offers then you need to be focusing on attending ten interviews which will certainly mean upwards of twenty applications.

The purpose of all this preamble is to get you to think about the number of positions which you need to identify through the media, and the volume of activity which you somehow need to generate (alongside your current job, and looking after the kids, and organising your partner's birthday party) in order to have a successful campaign. Three factors will help you:

Firstly the reality is that no job is as it is advertised and no company is as you first perceive it to be. So when you read job adverts don't look for reasons why you shouldn't apply because you are likely to apply for nothing. Consider instead the excuses which you have *for* applying.

A good example of this is location. This is important to all of us and it would be silly to discount it. By the same token, however, it would be foolish to ignore a job that was ideal in every respect other than its location without enquiring after it first. It may be they have other offices; the company will be moving in six months time; you might work from home and telecommute or even, contrary to what it says on the advert, they would consider paying relocation expenses to the right individual.

Secondly, organisations are more important than jobs. As you read the adverts you should consider that organisations have characters just as surely as people do. And, just as you would look for certain characteristics in a friend, so you should look for them in an organisation. Media corporations tend to be full of touchy feely types, with lots of parties and inter office affairs. Some love it, some hate it. Manufacturing organisations tend to fall into two categories: those which thrive on total chaos and disorganisation held together by a few key individuals who have generally been there for years, and those with high levels of investment operating within a world market and running on bright clean premises. Each attracts a different sort of individual. If you like the look of a company then apply. Use a covering letter to explain that you recognise your shortcomings relative to the ad requirements, and outline the reasons why you would like to be considered nonetheless. Remember, you need to keep your activity levels up to give yourself the choice you want. As they are recruiting anyway, there is every chance that they will have other positions more suitable to you.

The average number of responses to an advertised job in the US is in excess of 100. Many adverts however solicit no response at all! There is nothing more disheartening to a personnel department or agency than to advertise a job and get no response. You may not fit the bill exactly but if the response is poor then your c.v. will be welcomed whatever your experience.

Finally, use agents. I understand this book has an excellent list of them. Use them to widen your job search and maintain your activity levels. You will need to manage them accordingly. Arrange to meet, let them know that you are serious and get them to set themselves a target for dispatching your c.v. to various employers. Ring them up each week and check that they have done so and get their commitment to send it out again the following week. They earn a fee when you get a job so you are simply helping them to help themselves.

PETER BRUNSWICK *is a freelance career consultant. He is author of* The Recruitment Paradigm: How to move it to your advantage.

How To Get Promoted

CARLO LONGHI

Xerox

Moving your career forward doesn't have to mean leaving your current employer. An easier (and indeed better) alternative is to be promoted within the company you work for. Moving internally can be far less stressful than engaging external recruitment agencies and sitting through countless interviews, especially when the company and position which looked attractive from the outside prove to be a complete disaster once you're in.

The benefits of promotion within your current organisation often outweigh the "moving on" option. You already know how your organisation works, you know the people, the marketplace in which you operate, and you have firsthand experience of its pros and cons. All of this qualifies you to make an informed decision about your internal career prospects, compared to the relatively superficial information you are likely to obtain about a new company.

Moving within your current company will increase your breadth of knowledge across different facets of its business, while at the same time expanding your skills. As a result, your value to your employer is greatly increased.

At the same time you are expanding and growing your c.v. If the time does come for you to seek external employment, your broad and varied experience, combined with your proven company loyalty, may just give you the edge when up against stiff competition.

It is important to note that getting promoted may not necessarily mean an immediate vertical move. A horizontal shift which offers the opportunity for new experiences may be just as effective in helping you to reach your ultimate goal. Indeed, in some cases such a move may be a necessity.

The first thing to do when considering your prospects for promotion is to assess what skills and experience you have gained from both your previous and current job roles. Then formulate in your own mind a 3 to 5 year career plan. Consider with care anything beyond 5 years, as so many things might radically change in that time. Once you have evaluated the skills and experience you have against where you wish to take your career over the next five years, you can start to identify any gaps that need to be addressed. These gaps can be measured against any roles that exist within your current organisation. Don't necessarily look for job roles which are clearly vacant and need filling; the skills you wish to develop may comprise a role your employer has not even thought of yet.

At this point, you should be looking into as many different roles as possible. Even if you identify your ideal job, setting your sights on one role and putting all of your energy into pursuing it may mean bitter disappointment if for any reason you fail at the last hurdle. Instead, while keeping your fixed goal in mind, you should focus on two or three roles which look potentially interesting. Bear in mind that these may exist in areas of your organisation which, up until now, you have not previously considered. Stay open minded, and give yourself as many options as you can.

Once you have identified which two or three roles are of interest, you need to develop an action plan to help you land one of them. This may not be a short term campaign, and patience is the key. Most importantly, you must absolutely ensure that your plan is sound enough to support your ambition.

One of the first steps should include approaching the managers of those departments responsible for the roles you have identified, in order to register your interest. Engaging these departments may also uncover opportunities that you were previously unaware of, but which hold real appeal once you've discussed them in more detail. A role may well exist which was not apparent to you from the outside, but which offers your talents the opportunity to shine.

It is useful to have supporting documentation to leave with the head of the department, such as a c.v., a personal history form, achievement records, or third party references. These will be useful to help succinctly demonstrate your skills, achievements and experiences, and will leave a tangible impression on the person you've approached. Keep an Employee Development Record, updated on a regular basis, which will serve as an ideal vehicle for evidence statements.

In addition to registering your interest, this initial meeting will help you to establish what type of person the department wishes to recruit. This will allow you to match your current skills with the skills set they are looking for, while identifying any gaps you need to address. It may be prudent to also register your interest via the personnel department at this stage in order to ensure you are considered during any succession planning that may occur.

Having identified your targets, it is vital that you enlist the support of as many decision makers as possible. The more people you can get to speak for you in both formal and informal contact, the better. Don't be afraid to initiate some sort of appropriate contact with the manager's manager. They may help your cause by influencing from above. This exercise should also uncover any dissenters who may damage your chances. These people will be just as influential in your campaign, and it is important to establish what reservations they have so that you may address them.

Now that you have identified the roles you wish to pursue, and have spoken to the relevant people, you can progress with your plan of action. It should aim to fill the skills and knowledge gaps you have identified, as well as influencing your potential manager.

In order to ensure that you possess the skills you will need, consider adding to your experience through distance learning, night school, or self-teaching material. If you are considering a marketing role, for instance, but have very little or no marketing experience, you will need to go back to basics and learn the fundamentals of marketing. If you are considering moving in to a sales role, consider gaining some practical sales experience. Most of this activity will take place in your own time, but if it adds to your skills and helps you to achieve long-term goals, it is time well spent.

On a day-to-day basis seek to gain hands-on experience while making an impression on prospective managers. This is effectively achieved by involving yourself in cross-functional projects, which will close any skills gaps you still have, demonstrate your aptitude and provide supportive evidence at interview. Be proactive in project work. Don't coast along on the back of existing projects, but look for opportunities to run your own project team wherever possible. Demonstrate your leadership qualities and initiative.

While you should be focused on your goal, it is vital that you take a balanced approach. Don't get bogged down by taking on too much. Remember that you still need to perform well in your present job, and any tailing off in your performance will contradict everything you are trying to achieve. Be specific, and choose your route carefully. Your decisions should be governed by things that are going to give you direction, visibility, and build on your skills and knowledge base.

As your campaign progresses it is essential that you maintain all relevant contacts. Don't take it for granted that things you discussed six months go will still be the same today. Managerial requirements will change depending on the changing needs of the organisation. Managers may also change their opinions for a whole variety of reasons. By keeping abreast of those changes you will stay one step ahead of the competition.

By registering your interest, establishing your skills gaps and addressing them (via internal and external methods), demonstrating your aptitude in a variety of roles, getting involved in projects and work groups that are pertinent to your long-term ambitions, and maintaining contact with prospective managers, you will be giving yourself an ideal platform from which to progress within your current organisation.

Xerox is the leading provider of document processing solutions worldwide. CARLO LONGHI *is New Business Manager for Xerox Finance.*

Controlling the Interview

BRUCE MORTON

Alexander Mann Technology

There is a myth that the interview is not a selling situation. If you have any notion of subscribing to that belief stop reading this article right now!

The interview is possibly the least reliable way of assessing an individual's ability to do the job, but that's exactly how the vast majority of succesful candidates are chosen. Therefore it is essential that we learn some of the basic rules of winning the interview. In other words we learn how to sell ourselves in an interview situation.

PREPARATION:

You only get the one chance to impress, so the three most important elements of planning are Preparation, Preparation and Preparation.

1. Find out as much as you can about the organisation, with the amount of information that the Internet provides there can be no excuse for not being totally prepared in terms of company information.

2. Find out as much as you can about the actual position that you are being interviewed for. What are the actual duties and responsibilities of the position? What will be expected in tangible quantitative terms? What skills are essential in order to be successful in the role? Who currently holds this position? What are the future prospects? What are the minimum criteria for choosing an individual? This information will come from the recruitment company that is representing you, if they do not

have this information readily available you should insist that they get it. *You might also want to consider if this is the type of recruitment company that you want representing you.* If you have approached the company directly you should still endeavour to glean this information from within the organisation. The Marketing Department is usually a good initial point of contact.

3. Armed with this information you can start to plan for the interview in detail.

Fortunately there are standard questions that will be asked at the majority of interviews. I say fortunately because that means that you are able to plan your responses in advance. The classic questions are as follows:-

Why did you choose this particular industry/career?

What is it about our company that attracted you?

What do you want to be doing five years from now?

How do I manage you to get the very best from you?

What do you enjoy most about your current position?

What do you dislike about your current position?

What is your major strength?

What are you not so good at (weaknesses)?

What does teamwork mean to you?

What entrepreneurial activities have you been engaged in?

What skills can you bring to the organisation?

Why should we employ you?

What will your boss say when you hand in your notice?

It is important when preparing your responses that you do two things: always back up any statements that you make with factual examples; and always make sure you are pointing your responses to answer the requirements of the position.

For Example:

  The position calls for a lot of new business generation.

  Question: What do you dislike about your current position?

  Answer: There is too much *order taking* rather than being at the sharp end winning new business, where I really excel.

You should also prepare a list of questions to ask the interviewer. Classic examples are as follows:

Detailed information of the position.

Reason the position is available.

Induction and training programme.

Earnings of the most successful people in the same position in their third year.

  Company growth plans.

  Strategic plans for the future of the company.

  What criteria are the company using to choose the successful individual.

THE INTERVIEW:

It is vital that *you* take control of the interview. When I tell people this, the usual reaction is for people to say, "How can I control the interview when the interviewer is the one asking the questions?" In a way they have given themselves the answer. **He who asks the questions is in control!**

That is why it is essential that you are so well prepared that you can not only answer the interviewers questions, but also add a question to the end of the reply. In this way you maintain control.

For example:

Question : What do you enjoy most about your current position?

Answer: The most enjoyable part of my current role is the new business development. I really enjoy the challenge and buzz I get from winning a new account that I have generated from scratch. Tell me, what opportunity will I get to generate new business within this role?

By using this technique you will be able to direct which way the questioning goes. This will allow you to play to your strengths, as opposed to exposing any weaknesses that you may have in relation to the particular position.

It is far more effective to ask intelligent relevant questions to obtain the interviewers needs and then offer yourself as the solution rather than launch into a big sales pitch about how wonderful you are. Nobody likes a know-all. Everybody likes somebody who asks questions which allow them to celebrate themselves and their company.

THE CLOSE:

As this is a selling situation it is imperative that you close the interview as you would if you were selling a product or service (the product is you).

There are many different ways that you can bring the interview to a close, some of which I have listed below. The important thing is that you use words you are comfortable with. There can be no excuse for coming out of an interview not knowing how you have done. For the eight years that I was working as a recruitment consultant it never ceased to amaze me when a candidate would ask me after an interview, "How did I get on?" My response would be that there is somebody far better qualified than me to answer that question: the interviewer. Remember, the interviewer is looking for someone that can make things happen regardless of the position that you are being interviewed for.

Example closes:

"Do you have any reservations about my ability to do the job?"

If yes, what are they? This will give you the opportunity to overcome the objection there and then. It's too late once you have walked out of the interview, and the objection may simply be a misunderstanding.

"On a scale of one to ten how did you rate my ability to do the job?"

Anything below ten should then be qualified with

"What would I have to do to get a ten?"

"From the people that you have interviewed to date for this position, how do I fare?"

"If you did not have any more people to see would you be offering me the job?"

"If you were to offer me the position what training, if any, do you feel that I would need to be able to fulfil the role?"

If the interviewer is having a problem making his/her mind up or there are others involved in the decision making process a good question to ask is:

"What is your gut feeling?"

These fairly simplistic techniques have proved to be extremely successful. I have been coaching people from all walks of life in interview techniques for fourteen years now and the simple fact is the person that gets the job is the person who is the best interviewee. Your next interview could be the most influential hour of your life, take some time to prepare. Role play with your wife/husband/friend if possible. It will pay dividends.

BRUCE MORTON *is Managing Director of Alexander Mann Technology.*

The Recruitment Paradigm

PETER BRUNSWICK

Career Consultant

This article explains the paradigm which governs all recruitment at every level. Understand it and you will understand what you have to do to get the job you want. You can then take control of your career and set about obtaining the lifestyle you want.

Let me start by explaining what I mean by a paradigm. It is the set of rules both written and unwritten which govern our behaviour. When we walk along the road, people expect us to use the sidewalk. When we meet, we expect to shake hands, say good morning etc. These are the unwritten rules that make our lives easier and more comfortable. Recruitment, like every other area of human activity is also governed by its paradigms. Employers expect Interviewees to turn up appropriately dressed, and on time. They do not expect a butcher to apply for a nurse's job. Applicants too follow the same paradigms. When an advert asks for two years' experience, those with less will generally not apply.

Occasionally people break those rules. And when they do so they generally lose. A candidate turning up for interview for a senior executive role in torn jeans will not be invited back. And how many times have we heard that people are overqualified? Someone with a doctorate in medicine turning up to do a hospital auxiliary's job will be unsuccessful too. They are simply falling outside the expectations of those recruiting. Breaking a paradigm is a big no no. Shifting it, however, is another matter altogether.

Paradigm shifting is a big subject with hundreds of books written about it. In the corporate world it is a very important issue as many businesses get left behind in a changing world. Recognising that a paradigm has changed and responding to it is essential to corporate and human survival. Bill Gates, the founder of Microsoft refers to paradigm shifts as bends in the road. Microsoft nearly missed such a paradigm shift when it ignored the Internet in the early Nineties. Netscape among others had shifted the paradigms governing our communication behaviour firmly in favour of Internet technology. Microsoft had to react or die. Creating a paradigm shift and forcing others to react is one of the keys to winning in business. The same is true at interview.

If you were to plot a graph of presentation and interview skills on the y axis set against the relevant experience for a job along the x axis you would end up with a box into which those interviewing would expect the candidates to fit. Most candidates share those paradigms.

They expect to turn up in good time for the interview and to look presentable. This matches the interviewers expectations and represents the bottom side of the box. Anyone applying for an IT job will have some knowledge of IT. Interviewers would not expect a solicitor or baker to apply. This defines the left hand set of expectations. Over on the right, the interviewers are ideally hoping to meet someone who has done exactly the same job elsewhere, and done it well (why someone who is successful in one organisation should move to do the same job elsewhere is beyond me, but this is what employers hope for. They are doomed to be disappointed which is why interviewing is such a negative process. It is the job of a good recruitment consultant to reset their expectations to a lower level so that the interviewers are not disappointed). Nor will interviewers be expecting someone who has progressed beyond the advertised role to be applying. This represents the right hand side of the box.

The top right hand corner is the ideal location for any applicant. Anyone standing within it will have presented themselves well and will have just the sort of experience which the interviewer is looking for. Most of the other candidates will be randomly scattered inside the main box. Although they have all been credible candidates they will all be losers. *Anywhere inside the main set of paradigms which is not in the top right hand corner is a losing position.*

We've all been there. When we call for feedback we get lots of promising noises followed by the words, "but the competition was very strong and on this occasion we regret that we are unable to progress your application further."

And the real problem is that we can *never* be in the top right hand corner. After all most of us are changing jobs because we want to do something different, or want to get the promotion we were unable to secure in our current organisation. In other words there is an upper limit on your experience which is *always* going to be below the ideal sought by of the interviewers.

So given all that, is there a winning position which is not in the top right hand corner?

The answer is no, UNLESS you can move the corner such that no one else occupies it. The interviewers will then have to look within the larger box for their candidate. And this is what we mean by shifting the paradigm.

I can guarantee that you have all seen it done before. How many times have you seen a job being advertised internally where the right candidate has been obvious from the start. When that happens we often wonder why anyone should bother applying, since our colleague seems to have the job in the bag already. Then they announce the winner and it is.... not your colleague but someone completely unexpected.

Suddenly we're all running round yelling, "Have you heard who got the job" and, "Did you know they gave it to such and such" and, "I can't believe it." Unexpected people get the promotions because they succeed in shifting the interviewers' paradigms. It happens all the time. Let's see how you could do it too.

There are actually hundreds of ways of shifting the recruitment paradigm, many of which are explained in my book. A method favoured by recruitment consultants is to begin the wash-up meeting by discussing the worst candidate interviewed. This resets the employer's expectations downwards and every other candidate suddenly looks a lot better.

What I am about to describe next, however, is one of the simplest and most powerful ways of shifting a recruitment paradigm and is applicable for just about any role.

Begin by taking a blank sheet of paper and draw a vertical line down the middle. Head one side 'Requirements' and head the other 'Evidence'. Now write down the first thing they want under Requirements. Maybe it is Managerial Experience. On the other side write down what experience you have. "But I have none", I hear you say. Rubbish. Almost all the candidates I have ever met under sell themselves. You may be a mother returning to work, in which case you have piles of management experience. You've managed the family finance, got the kids to school in the morning, the continuous house moves in support of your husband's career. Maybe you have none of that. If the only thing you have ever managed has been the organising of the Christmas party, or the local school sports day, then get it down. Remember that the issues you had to address then, organising and motivating individuals, will be no different to those you will have to address as a manager.

Then move onto the next requirement.

Interpersonal skills: tell them about your involvement in the local cricket club

Disciplined approach to work: tell them about your research for the job you are applying for.

Programming experience: get some examples of your work together.

Soon you should have a list of all the things which they are looking for, each one set against an example which demonstrates that you meet that requirement. It is essential to address every one of their requirements. If the person interviewing you has to justify their choice to their manager it is important that they can answer every concern regarding you as a candidate.

Now consider what the job would involve.

Again make two columns, one headed Requirement the other headed Action. You might call this your Business Plan. Its about showing what you would do were you given the job, and showing that you are capable of doing it.

One aspect of an IT role might be to take responsibility for documenting system changes. Think about how you would do that. One of the things you might do to start with is get familiar with the systems. On its own that is a little bit wishy washy. You could support it by giving a time scale by which you would expect to be familiar with the systems. Detail who you might need to speak to in order to find out about the systems and when you expect to have done that. If you contacted the Sales office as part of your research for the role, then you can demonstrate that you have already completed the first part of that process. It is always difficult to think clearly in an interview so *write it down*.

Now type it up, print it out and bind it. Three copies. Give it a title: Application of [name] for [position] of... etc and date it. Now I will make you a promise:

If you walk into an interview and put the three copies on the table the first thing that the interviewer will say is, "What is that?"

Then you say, "I wanted to be as prepared as possible so I just took a few minutes to gather all my thoughts on paper." Then give them a choice, "I was going to leave it with you but we could go through it now if you would rather."

Can you feel that paradigm shifting?

Ninety nine times out of a hundred they will take the easy option. They don't want to have to ask questions. OK then, lets see what you've got. The floor is now yours. You have full control of the interview process. You have the material you require, with one copy for you and one for each of the interviewers. You may now proceed to reset their expectations in your favour.

By demonstrating a thoroughness and professionalism beyond the expected you have forced them to consider you for the job. Even if someone else is better qualified and more experienced, they will at the very least invite you back for a second interview. Almost without fail, the other candidate, who still doesn't realise that the paradigms have shifted will make a lower impression next time round. They will never get into the top right hand corner. You, on the other hand, know the score and can improve on your last performance. Anyone failing to meet your standards will appear wan and lacklustre.

By the finish of the second interview it is a no-brainer. We were very impressed by your presentation, and we would like to offer you the job. Yes, yes, yeeessss! yippee, fantastic. You punch the air, kiss your partner and dance around the room. It feels better than sex.

The above is just one, albeit very powerful, way of shifting an employers paradigms. There are hundreds but they all have a common thread: preparation.

PETER BRUNSWICK *is a freelance career consultant. He is author of* The Recruitment Paradigm: How to move it to your advantage.

Answering Tough Interview Questions

AMY ROWSON

Marks and Spencer

When attending an interview, the first thing to remember is the purpose of the interview itself: mutual marketing, assessment and fact-finding. The interviewers want to sell the company and the position to you, and you want to sell yourself as the ideal candidate. They want to evaluate your skills, and you want to present them in the most positive way possible. Their aim is to find out more about you, just as you want to learn more about them. Remembering that the interview is a two-way process is a good way to help you to prepare, and being prepared will help you to be positive and in control.

An important aspect of developing a good interview technique is to learn to be brief and to the point. The interviewers are looking for a great deal of information in a short space of time, so present your replies clearly and succinctly. Certain questions are formulated to give you the opportunity to describe situations which give the interviewers evidence of your skills and abilities. Be ready to assess your own skills, and have examples of a range of situations where you've put them to good use. Two important points to remember are not to put anything down on the application form which you cannot substantiate at interview, and not to lie.

Of course, there is always going to be an element of surprise in the interview process. There are certain questions designed to catch you off guard and make you think on your feet. We want to assess your judgement and intellectual depth, and we have developed questions which test these traits. So how do you prepare yourself to answer such questions? The following will give you an idea of what you're likely to be asked, and what we hope to learn from your responses.

Expect to be asked questions which take you away from your knowledge/experience base. We want to see evidence of your comprehension, analysis, and evaluation. The best way for us to test these is to take you out of your own realm. We may challenge your ideas with a reasonable opposing view. This isn't personal, nor should you assume we disagree or disapprove of the position you've taken. We wish to observe your reactions and your ability to maintain your own position. We often use questions which contain two parts, to see if you distinguish and adequately address both. In such cases you should aim to think through these questions thoroughly and give a considered, concise response. A favourite question is to ask your views on a current affairs issue, and then ask you to justify your views. We are looking for evidence of the depth of your thinking, and your ability to justify an opinion.

Using examples from your own experience, we will want to know why you made certain choices, what you've learned from those experiences, and what, with hindsight, you would change. This gives us some measure of your analytical ability. Another way of judging the same thing is to get you to explain, in simple terms, the rules of a board game, or to have you give a synopsis of a course you've done.

To evaluate your judgement, we might ask you to identify your strongest attributes, or to evaluate your performance in a given situation. Then we will ask you to solve a problem, who your role model is and why, what you have to offer the company, or how you dealt with something unexpected.

We also want to evaluate your capacity for ownership and commitment to a position. You may be asked where you see yourself in a few years time, what motivates you, what your ambitions are, and why you've chosen your career. We will then ask for examples of projects you've committed to and seen through.

Depending on the position you're being interviewed for, we sometimes ask questions which determine whether you have the courage of your convictions. We ask you for your views about a particular issue then take an opposing view.

Or we might ask what you have done in a situation where you disagreed with someone or something, or were forced to take an unpopular stance.

A quality many companies search for in their candidates is effective leadership. Providing past examples is good evidence, but you will probably be asked to go into some detail about the qualities which made you a good leader: organising, motivating, disciplining, raising standards, etc. Think of individuals with strong leadership ability (no points for Blair/Hague/Ashdown) and use them to evidence your answers. You may be asked how you have motivated a lazy team member, or convinced someone to do a job they did not want to do.

Your teamwork skills will almost certainly be questioned at interview, so it is an area which is worth some extra preparation. The achievements and failures of teams you have been in will be discussed. We want to know how well you work with others and where you fit into the team mix. Awareness of the various team roles and their functions, and which of these has characterised your past performance, is very valuable. We want to find out how you would perform in negative situations as well as positive ones by asking how you've reacted when your pet proposal was rejected by your team, or why a team you have been a part of was unsuccessful or ineffective. We are not questioning the effectiveness of your past experiences but assessing how you have behaved in a variety of situations.

Another area we want to look at is your interpersonal skills. We establish these by asking how you have dealt with difficult people, what you feel passionately about, how you have responded to past criticism, what your greatest achievements and responsibilities have been, or which of your personal qualities have improved over time. We look for evidence that you are a rounded person, and want to know about your hobbies and outside interests. Essentially, we are want evidence of your personal development and ability to get on with people.

While this list is by no means comprehensive, it aims to give you a good sense of what we are trying to learn from you. During your interview preparation, concentrate on the areas I've outlined. This will help you to determine what line the interviewer is pursuing, and formulate an appropriate answer.

A few more basic tips about interview technique will give you a framework for your preparation. Try to remain relaxed and enthusiastic. If you've made it to the interview you're already halfway to succeeding. Be direct and concise. If you've done your preparation, you'll already have a good idea of what you want to say. Remember to be specific, and try not to let yourself ramble. The interview should feel like a conversation, with input from both sides.

If the interviewer does ask a question which stumps you, or that you haven't thought of, take your time before replying. A thoughtful and considered reply will be better received than a quick, garbled one. If you do need a minute to think, tell the interviewer. Merely sitting in silence may convey the impression that your nerves have got the better of you. If you say something like, "That's an interesting question. Let me take a minute to think about how best to answer it", you will buy the time you need while still appearing confident and in control. Don't be afraid to ask for clarification if you feel that a question has not been specific enough.

If you are faced with an interviewer who seems aggressive or difficult, remain calm, pleasant and professional throughout. They may simply be trying to assess different aspects of your personality, or gauge your reactions to certain kinds of behaviour. Don't let this throw you. Remember that a warm smile can have a very positive effect, even on the most seasoned interviewer.

After the interview, it is useful to give yourself a bit of a de-briefing session. Review your performance and think about which questions you found tough. Could you have prepared better for them? Is there any way you could prepare better next time? If the questions were tough because you found them too technical, it may be that you were applying for a position which falls outside your current area of expertise. If you found them too probing, and they required more detail than you were able to give, it may be that you have not prepared well enough or that you have exaggerated some of your skills. You may want to re-evaluate the way you have presented your previous experience.

It is important to learn from the interview. If you are asked to come in for a second interview, it is vital that you review your performance in the first. The second interview is likely to be even more specific, so if you want to be successful you have to do your homework.

Remember that no one is perfect, especially the interviewer. You can make their job easier, and greatly improve your own chances of success, by being prepared, concise, direct, and confident.

Marks and Spencer is one of Britain's best known and most respected brand names. AMY ROWSON *is the Assistant Graduate Attraction Manager.* Tests and Assessments: Examples

Tests and Assessments

MICK SMITH

De Montfort University

Selecting the right person for any job is a tricky business. Employers must determine which of the aspiring candidates will be the most likely to fit, not just in terms of their **eligibility**, i.e. their qualifications and experience, but also their **suitability**, i.e. their personality profile and likely compatibility with existing members of a team. In a situation where an employer has a large pool of eligible candidates to choose from, such as entry onto corporate graduate training programmes, then measures of suitability and personality take on a particular significance.

In recent years a considerable market has grown up offering employers means of assessing job candidates; some of these are highly reputable and sound, and some are less so. The reputable tests, such as the ones described below, have been developed and refined over a period of many years and are supported by detailed published information concerning their **validity** and **reliability** in different contexts. (Validity refers to a test's ability to measure the factor it was designed to measure, reliability gauges the consistency of a test's results). Good employers use selection tests as tools in conjunction with other selection processes, and assessors understand the strengths and the limitations of the tools they use. They help employers to make a fairer and more informed decisions about selecting the right candidate for the job.

Examples of Tests that can be used for Selection Purposes.

THE 16PF TEST

The Sixteen Personality Factor Questionnaire is published by ASE, a Division of NFER-Nelson. It represents Dr. Raymond Cattells endeavour to identify the primary components of personality analysing all English language adjectives describing human behaviour. The fifth edition, updated and revised, continues to measure the same 16 primary factor scales identified by Dr Cattell over 45 years ago. In addition, the primary factors are clustered into broad personality domains called Global Factors.

The questionnaire, which can be administered individually or in a group setting, takes 35 to 50 minutes to complete by hand or 25 to 35 minutes to complete when administered as part of ASEs Screen-Test psychometric software system. It can easily be scored with a set of keys, a process normally taking approximately 15 minutes per candidate.

The 16PF is un-timed, but you are encouraged to work at a steady pace and to give the first natural answer as it comes to you. The 185 questions have a three choice response format. For most the middle response is a question mark and you are encouraged to chose between a) or c) as in the examples below:

Examples:

I often like to watch team games

a) true   b) ?   c) false

I prefer friends who are:

a) quiet   b) ?   c) lively

As a broad measure of personality, the 16PF is useful in a variety of settings to predict a wide range of behaviours and is a highly respected test.

Table 1.

Primary Factor Scale Descriptors for the UK Edition of the 16PF5®

	Factor	Left Meaning	Right Meaning
A	Warmth	More emotionally distant from People	Attentive and Warm to Others
B	Reasoning	Fewer Reasoning Items Correct	More Reasoning Items Correct
C	Emotional Stability	Reactive, Emotionally Changeable	Emotionally Stable, Adaptive
E	Dominance	Deferential, Cooperative, Avoids Conflict	Dominant, Forceful
F	Livliness	Serious, Cautious, Careful	Lively, Animated, Spontaneous
G	Rule Consciousness	Expedient, Non-conforming	Rule-conscious, Dutiful
H	Social Boldness	Shy, Threat-sensitive, Timid	Socially Bold, Venturesome
I	Sensitivity	Objective, Unsenimental	Subjective, Sentimental
L	Vigilance	Trusting, Unsuspecting, Accepting	Vigilant, Suspicious, Sceptical, Wary
M	Abstractedness	Grounded, Practical, Solution-orientated	Abstracted, Theoretical
N	Privateness	Forthright, Straightforward	Private, Discreet, Non-disclosing
O	Apprehension	Self-assured, Unworried	Apprehensive, Self-doubting, Worried
Q1	Openness to Change	Traditional, Values the Familiar	Open to Change Experimenting
Q2	Self-reliance	Group-orientated, Affiliative	Self-reliant, Individualistic
Q3	Perfectionism	Tolerates Disorder, Unexacting, Flexible	Self-disciplined, Perfectionistic Organized
Q4	Tension	Relaxed, Placid, Patient	Tense, High Energy, Impatient, Driven

THE MYERS-BRIGGS TYPE INDICATOR®

Oxford Psychologists Press are the exclusive licencees for the Myers-Briggs Type Indicator in the UK. It derives from and extends Carl Jungs famous work on Types. Isabel Myers and her mother Katherine Briggs modified and clarified Jungs ideas into a framework which was further painstakingly tested and refined by Isabel Myers. Now after more than fifty years it is translated into other languages, cultures or settings and is the most widely used personality indicator in the world.

In essence the MBTI® identifies a person's preferences, elements of the personality which may be expressed in terms of four key pairs of preferences (see table 2). Each preference is designated by a letter and they interact with each other to form 16 different combinations: for example, ISTJ, (which is one of the most frequently occurring types in top management in many countries, including the UK), ENFP, INTP, etc.

The MBTI can be administered individually or in a group setting and usually takes 15 – 25 minutes to complete. As with the 16 PF it is hand scored using a set of keys, a process taking approximately 5 minutes. The questionnaire is un-timed and you are encouraged to respond spontaneously to the 88 multiple choice questions. For example:

Would you rather work with someone who is

        a) always kind, or
        b) always fair

On most matters, do you

        a) have a pretty definite opinion
        b) like to keep an open mind

Table 2: What the MBTI Measures:

The MBTI describes an individuals preferences on four independent dimensions. The person is either:

E	Extroverted	Prefers to focus on the outer world of people and things
or		
I	Introverted	Focuses on the inner world of ideas and impressions
S	Sensing	Focuses on the present and on information gained from their senses
or		
N	Intuitive	Focuses on the future, on patterns and possibilities
T	Thinking	Bases decisions on logic and objective analysis of cause and effect
or		
F	Feeling	Bases decisions primarily on values and subjective evaluation of person centred concerns
J	Judging	Likes a planned, organised approach to life and prefers to have things settled
or		
P	Perceiving	Likes a flexible, spontaneous approach and prefers to keep options open

The MBTI is use primarily for personal and team development, but you may encounter it in selection processes. It is an extremely useful tool that highlights constructive aspects of differences between people and which can help to identify and develop individual strengths as well as manage particular weaknesses. If you complete the questionnaire seek specific feedback relative to your personal profile.

THE BELBIN TEAM ROLE PROFILE

Dr Meredith Belbin has spent over twenty years studying management teams. He asserts that what makes a person right for a job or team role depends a great deal on the shape of the person and their fit with the other people in the team. A well-composed, well-constructed team will out-perform even the most able individual. In his research Belbin isolated and identified nine team roles (see table 3). The Questionnaire, first published in Management Teams *(1981, Butterworth Heinemann ISBN 0-7506-2676-3)* enables respondents to identify which of these they have a preference towards, which they can undertake reasonably comfortably, and which they should try and avoid.

The Belbin questionnaire takes about 15 – 20 minutes to complete, individually or in a group setting. It can be scored by computer using the Belbin Interplace Computer System. The advantage of the latter is that it produces detailed personal feedback and allows for respondents to check out their self-perceptions regarding their profiles in relation to the perceptions of other team members.

The test is un-timed and spontaneous answers are called for. There are seven sections. In each section you would need to distribute 10 points among the sentences which you think best describe your behaviour, or how you see yourself.

For example:
What I believe I can contribute to a team is that…

Table 3: Roles and Descriptions

PLANT: Creative, imaginative, unorthodox. Solves difficult problems. **Allowable weaknesses:** Weak in communicating with and managing ordinary people.

RESOURCE INVESTIGATOR: Extrovert, enthusiastic, communicative. Explores opportunities. Develops contacts. **Allowable weaknesses:** Loses interest once initial enthusiasm has passed.

CO-ORDINATOR: Mature, confident and trusting. A good chairman. Clarifies goals, promotes decision making. **Allowable weaknesses:** Not necessarily the most clever or creative member of a group.

SHAPER: Dynamic, outgoing, highly strung. Challenges, pressures, finds ways round obstacles. **Allowable weaknesses:** Prone to provocation and short-lived bursts of temper.

MONITOR EVALUATOR: Sober, strategic, and discerning. Sees all options. Judges accurately. **Allowable weaknesses:** Lacks drive and ability to inspire others.

TEAMWORKER: Social, mild, perceptive and accommodating. Listens, builds, averts friction. **Allowable weaknesses:** Indicisive in crunch situations.

IMPLEMENTER: Disciplined, reliable, conservative and efficient. Turns ideas into practical actions. **Allowable weaknesses:** Somewhat inflexible, slow to respond to new possibilities.

COMPLETER: Painstaking, concientious, anxious. Turns ideas into practical actions. **Allowable weaknesses:** Inclined to worry unduly, reluctant to delegate.

SPECIALIST: Single-minded, self-starting, dedicated. Provides knowledge or technical skills in rare supply. **Allowable weaknesses:** Contributes only on a narrow front.

a) I think I can work quickly to take advantage of new opportunities.

b) I can work well with a very wide range of people.

Belbin's framework is used extensively in the selection process to help identify the candidate's likely area of team role contribution, and the extent to which this will complement the profile of the existing team. Knowing your Belbin team role profile is useful for an employer wishing to assess suitability. A candidate who volunteers a clear profile will often prompt an employer to consider them for a vacancy which has not yet been advertised.

THE OPQ® (OCCUPATIONAL PERSONALITY QUESTIONNAIRE)

Since its launch in 1984 the OPQ has quickly become the UKs most popular personality questionnaire. Developed by Professor Peter Saville and Roger Holdsworth in the early eighties it was the first mainstream test designed specifically for the UK. Launched in 1984 by SHL its astonishing success opened up the UK market. It has gone on to become available in over 25 languages and is becomming very popular as a tool for international assessment. The OPQ was designed to be a constantly evolving family of instruments always being expanded and further developed.

The OPQ gives information about an individuals personal qualities and the way they go about things. It assesses their style rather than ability and there are no right or wrong answers. It therefore typically forms only part of an assessment to be interpreted alongside other information. It is a very flexible tool and as a consequence it is used in a wide range of situations. Candidates may well also come across it in training and counselling situations.

The OPQ measures a number of characteristics (or preferred style of behaving) which affect an individuals performance at work including:

> relationships with people
> thinking and problem solving style
> emotions, motivation and drive
> leadership or subordinate styles
> selling and influencing styles.

There are 8 different versions of the OPQ. All of them ask questions about how an individual typically behaves at work. There is no time limit for completion but to ensure that the answers best reflect an individual it is best to work quickly through them rather than pondering at length over any one question. The answers are then used to produce a profile of how the individual sees themselves compared to a group of similar individuals.

Doing Well at Assessment Centres

MIKE BORROW

British Aerospace

The idea of attending an assessment centre can be extremely intimidating. What is involved? What are the assessors looking for? How do you ensure that you present yourself in the right way? In this article I hope to give some specific answers to these questions.

Though they vary from company to company, the purpose of the assessment is always the same: to test a number of candidates, both individually and in groups, in a variety of controlled situations. It also offers the company a chance to sell itself to you, and it is likely that time will be set aside to do this.

The assessment centre obviously lasts much longer than the traditional interview, and for good reason. Interviews are recognised as being pretty poor predictors of a candidates eventual job performance. Assessment centres, on the other hand, allow the employer to view candidates in a variety of situations, giving a more rounded and realistic view of an individuals strengths. The activities in which candidates will take part are structured around a set of competencies, which the employer has identified as important to successful job performance. Role-playing, group discussions, aptitude tests, team building, and interviews are all likely to feature including elements of fact finding, problem solving, and teamwork.

Of all the areas likely to be tested, teamwork is the most significant. Employers want to see that you can work well within a team, performing effectively without domineering or stifling the other members. This is an important skill to have, and a difficult one to fake even for a short time, so its something worth working on. It is also a skill for which written tests and one-to-one interviews offer no measure of ability, so assessment centres tend to overflow with teamwork exercises. To succeed in these it is worth remembering the following:

Although you are clearly competing for one of a limited number of positions, too much competition within a teamwork exercise can stifle the dynamics to the detriment of everyone. It is better to focus your competitiveness and that of your colleagues outside of the group. This may seem difficult at first, but remember that the assessment centre is likely to divide candidates into several groups. Focus on trying to beat the other teams. This is far more likely to win approval than attempting to compete for control and attention within your own group.

The assessors will want to see evidence of good leadership. Remember that the best leadership is often understated. The brash team member who loudly espouses his own views may well attract attention, but it may not be the sort he was looking for. If anyone attempts to take control early on, don't be tempted into an obvious and unproductive power struggle. Lead from within, make positive contributions, listen to others and try to involve the less forthright team members in decisions.

Occasionally, teams don't work out for one reason or another. Remember that problem solving of this nature is one of the skills which you should be able to demonstrate, but if you really feel that some aspect of the team's performance is seriously affecting its ability to work effectively, talk to the assessors. Explain the problem and list what you have done to try and resolve it. Then ask for suggestions from the assessor. They may be able to help, but even if they can't you have made them aware of the problem in relatively positive terms.

In an assessment centre (unlike in real life) the way in which the team has gone about achieving the task is as important as the task itself. Be careful about sacrificing the group dynamic, or the input and feelings of individual members, to the overall outcome. Employers recognise that teams which work well inevitably achieve better results than those that don't. Concentrate on the teamwork and the results will follow.

A few more general tips will probably help your overall performance. Assessment centres are designed to stretch your abilities, so it is likely to be a demanding experience. Try to stay calm and relaxed, and enjoy the experience as much as you can. Don't forget why you are there. If the assessment lasts for several days, you will be under observation all the time. Whether you're sitting next to the Head of Personnel at dinner or chatting to another candidate in the loo, don't say or do anything which might jeopardise your chances.

The company will probably make a presentation at the beginning of the assessment process, in which it markets itself to you. There are several ways to use this to your advantage. It is an ideal opportunity to learn about the company's culture, and get a sense of the atmosphere you would be working in. You should assess these things as carefully as you would any other aspect of the job, as your future with the company depends on you fitting in well with its established culture. You should have done some research into the company's background, and this is a perfect opportunity to ask any questions you may have. The company has allocated time and effort to sell themselves to you, so let them know it's been time well spent. Be attentive, responsive, and offer positive feedback. When the assessment activities begin, they will remember you.

BAe Systems is Britain's biggest manufacturing exporter, Europe's largest defence company and a major force in the commercial airliner industry. MIKE BORROW is Young People Resourcing Manager.

Effective Teamwork

TOM WILLIAMS

Saatchi and Saatchi

In a business environment, what is that one elusive thing that marks out one group of people from another?

It's not how intelligent they all are. It's not how similar they are to each other. It's not even how well they like each other. It's how well they work together.

It's how well they become so much more than the sum of their component parts, to become one single effective and dynamic professional unit. It's how well they become one team and not ten individuals.

The reason for this is very simple. Although leaders are needed in a team, the group of ten outspoken individuals who find it hard to follow one another's lead or to accept one another's point of view, will not become a team. Although mediators are needed in a team, the group of ten conciliatory individuals who can only contribute through reconciling opposing opinions into what is at best a compromise will not become a team. Although thinkers are needed in a team, the group of ten silent individuals who need stimulus from others before they can develop a strategy or proposal through quiet, solitary reflection will not become a team. And although doers are needed in a team, the group of ten hyperactive individuals who contribute only through running about implementing the direction of others will not become a team.

The best teams are made up by people who are *not* alike: different roles within the group dynamic demand different characters amongst the component personnel. And if one or more of the parts are missing then the team is incomplete and will fail.

Teams have to be *built*, thought through and planned before they can function. Just as all the mechanical parts of a car have to be in place before it can be driven, or all the organs in a body have to be pumping for life to be sustained, so a team is forever dependent on all factors within it being healthy, present and correct.

A company is just another word for a team. And Advertising Agencies, such as the company that I work for, are extreme examples of this. Many businesses are concerned with balancing the bottom line or increasing profit margins, challenges which can largely be attained by following a rigid, tried-and-tested organisational structure with reliance on hardware and machinery to actually make the product. If the machines in the factory break down, productivity is disrupted.

In advertising and other sides of the media industry, the factory machine is the team assigned to the business. These people become the production line of strategies, creative executions and media plans. It is as crucial that this machine does not break down as it is essential that the transistors and microchips on the computer-making machine are kept in order.

The same principles to maintenance of the machines apply in both instances. The parts must be the right ones to begin with, fresh and ready for the clearly-signalled task in hand. They must work in harmony with all the other parts within the machine, must receive regular checks and servicing and must all realise that if one part breaks down then there is no purpose in them powering on to prove a point; they must help to repair the broken part before the process can continue.

Nowhere is this more apparent than in the job that I do, and I hope that a brief explanation of the advertising process will clarify why an interview for a job in an advertising agency will spend a perfunctory amount of time examining individual talent and yet will study the candidate's performance in a group environment for hour after hour.

Just as in other businesses, the Advertising Agency's product is the result of the combined efforts of a number of people with wide ranging skills and personalities. And in an agency of some size, the core team responsible for delivering this is often made up of leaders or representatives of smaller, internal teams that in turn have to deliver a product to their client, namely the core team.

The core team structure of an agency is very similar to a Venn Diagram. A large circle in the middle signifies the management team and the smaller circles that adjoin at various points around the perimeter are sub-teams that make contributions to the final project. Wheels on the management team's chassis, if you like.

For each project within the agency, whether it be a television commercial for a brand of lager or a live poster featuring Melinda Messenger promoting a certain brand of shampoo, there is a core management team in place. That team taps into the resource of the whole agency to varying degrees depending on the demands of the situation as determined by the Account Manager. Some accounts may only require a Toyota Starlet of a team. Others may need the full Previa.

The process starts when a client decides to ask you to develop some advertising or piece of communications to help promote their product/service/image. The Account Manager meets the client and receives a brief of what is required.

They then return to the agency and put a team in place that they feel will best meet the demands of this new account. It will be dependent on the character of the client (are they easy-going or are they perfectionists who need all the t's crossed?), the nature of the product and how it will be advertised (is it a product-demonstration shampoo, an image-led car brand, or something that requires more tactical stunt advertising?), the timings (are they busy? on a training course? on holiday?) and past experience (do I work well with them?).

With the group of individuals in place, the Account Manager can then set about making them into a team. The other sub-teams contribute active elements of the final product, such as a strategy and a creative idea. The Account Manager's product is a guarantee that the team will be managed well enough that each element will perform to their optimum level and that their individual actions will ultimately combine to give a bit of magic to the communications. In short that the end will be greater than the sum of its parts. A bit like a coach in a football game.

Consider the other positions. In central mid-field the strategic planning element sets the pace, determining how and where the product should be positioned and viewed within the market place. Once they have determined a proposition (e.g. for Club 18-30 holidays the proposition was, "Go on a holiday your mother wouldn't approve of.") they pass the ball forward to the dazzling strike duo, the copy writer and the art director that make up the creative team who will be charged with making it happen. They'll be brought up to speed on the current thinking of the team and asked to go away and determine the most relevant and interesting way in which this idea could be conveyed to the relevant target audience.

The creatives will hammer the ball brilliantly into the back of the net (for Club 18-30: Beaver Espana etc.), and will then need support from the solid back line of the production team (how are we going to make this ad?) and the media team (where are people going to see this ad?). All the while the timings and budgets and overall team performance are being overseen by the Account Manager who, whilst not actually involved on the pitch, monitors the players and rings the changes if need be.

This is what effective teamwork is about, and how it is most commonly perceived on a day to day basis. A goalkeeper, a defender, a striker and a coach all contribute to the team performance in different ways. One player may be under-performing, so perhaps he should move to the left side of mid-field, or be taken off the pitch for a while. The team may be under-performing, so maybe the coach needs to switch to playing wing-backs instead of your conventional four 4-4-2. Even the physio is the most important player in the stadium when your 18 year-old golden boy goes down with a thigh strain.

In advertising and in business, just as in football, you aren't judged on whether you can kick a good penalty, or whether you can run 100m quicker than the next man. In interviews you will be tested to see whether you have the vision to deliver the right pass to the right man at the right time, or whether you're prepared to cover back 50 yards when one of your team-mates is caught short and a possible breach in the defences is on the cards.

In football you are never more than one man within a squad, one player within a team. The same applies for business. More so. When money counts, it's no longer just a game.

Saatchi and Saatchi London is the flagship agency of Saatchi and Saatchi Worldwide, a network encompassing offices in 91 countries. It is the world's most creative ideas company. TOM WILLIAMS *is an Account Supervisor.*

Numerical and Reasoning Tests

VERBAL TESTS

This test assesses the ability to organize verbal information in the way that makes the most sense and has the greatest logical structure. In each question you are presented with a passage of prose consisting of four sentences in which the original order of the sentences has been changed.

Your task is to read through the sentences in each set to get a sense of the passage, and then determine the correct sequence of the sentences.

You should allow yourself approximately 2 minutes to complete the following 2 questions.

Question 1:

A) She approached the door with caution, her heartbeat accelerating. B) As she got out of her chair she wondered who it could be at this time of night. C) The piercing sound of the doorbell made her jump. D) She was much relieved to find it was only her neighbour asking to borrow a cup of sugar.

Question 2:

A) All that is left for you to do then is to wait for the plane and there will normally be refreshments available to help you pass the time. B) Upon arrival you should check in at the front desk at least one hour before your plane is scheduled to leave. C) Before leaving for the airport you should check that you have your tickets, passport and currency. D) You will hand over your luggage at the desk although you will normally be allowed to retain one small piece of hand luggage.

NUMERICAL TEST (A)

This test assesses the ability to understand numerical data presented in tables and other formats and to make rapid decisions based upon such information. It provides an assessment of your numerical awareness. Some basic calculation is involved but little arithmetic skill or mathematical knowledge is required. To perform well, you need to be able to select and manipulate the relevant data from a complex data set to decide on the correct answer.

For each question you are required to select the correct answer from five possible alternatives which are provided.

You will need to be able to work out percentages in order to answer some of the questions in this test, and practice may be useful. Please note that, for this test, the potential benefit to you of guessing increases in relation to the number of the potential answers you are able to eliminate. If, for example, you can reduce the number of realistic options to two, then you will benefit from guessing between these two.

Table 1:

Percentage increase in weekly prices since 1992

Average family expenditure and % Increase on 1992 rate

Product	92	93	94	95	96	97
Food	£70	2.3	4.8	7.8	11.6	15.6
Alcohol	£10	0.3	2.3	7.9	17.1	21.7
Housing	£45	3.3	8.4	14.0	20.5	28.5
Fuel	£12	1.3	6.0	9.9	14.5	20.9
Transport	£18	0.5	0.5	2.1	6.7	9.9
Clothing	£12	2.0	3.5	4.9	7.0	9.9
Others	£36	0.2	1.8	3.4	7.2	11.0

The use of calculators is not permitted during this test. You should allow yourself approximately 5 minutes to complete the following 3 questions.

Question 3:

If the average family bought the same food in 1996 as they did in 1992, approximately how much would their weekly food bill cost in 1996?

A) £78.10   B) £75.69   C) £81.13   D) £81.60   E) £79.85

Question 4:

If the Lee family buy 15% more clothing and 5% less food than the average family, by approximately how much will their bill differ from that of the average family in 1992?

A) –£2.13   B) –£0.09   C) –£1.70   D) +£1.60   E) +£2.13

Question 5:

If the average family income was £196 in 1992 and has increased by 25% in 1997, approximately how much will the average family have after paying for housing and fuel?

A)£151.63   B)£158.00   C)£170.20   D)£172.67   E)£198.00

NUMERICAL TEST (B)

This test is a measure of logical and flexible reasoning ability on a task requiring discovery of missing elements in sets of numbers. The test assesses capacity to appreciate numerical relationships, to identify logical principles and to move easily between detection strategies.

Each question comprise a set of numbers where one number is missing and has been replaced with XX. In all cases the answer is a two digit number.

Your task is to work out which is the correct answer to each question and then record your answer on the answer sheet by filling in the circle next to the letter associated with answer of your choice.

Try the following questions. You should allow yourself approximately 4½ minutes to complete these questions.

Question 6:

	3	10	XX	24	31

A) 12   B) 17   C) 19   D)16   E) 13

Question 7:

	36	28	22	XX	16

A) 20   B) 21   C) 18   D)15   E) 14

Question 8:

	1	2	6	XX	120

A) 20   B) 10   C) 60   D) 72   E) 24

Question 9:

	4589	23XX	3478	1256

A) 67   B) 76   C) 45   D) 56   E) 84

Question 10:

	6	8	12	XX	26

A) 22   B) 14   C) 16   D)18   E) 24

Question 11:

	36	29	24	XX	20

A) 21   B) 19   C) 23   D) 20   D)22

Question 12:

	14418	19221	22527	172XX	19928

A) 36   B) 19   C) 26   D) 15   E) 30

Question 13:

    92   XX   40   86   50   36

A) 72   B) 56   C) 52   D) 48   E) 62

LOGICAL REASONING – TYPE A

There are two sorts of logical reasoning tests. The questions in this test measure the ability to identify the meaning in verbally complex material and to distinguish what is implied from what is actually stated.

The questions are presented in groups of three, preceded by a passage of information. You should assume that the information given in the passage is completely true. Each passage is followed by three statements. Your task is to say, given the information in the passage, whether each statement is definitely true (True), definitely false (False) or whether it is not possible to say that it is definitely one or the other (Maybe).

Please note that for Type A questions a proportion of the score is deducted for incorrect answers. Caution should be exercised with regard to guessing at answers.

Try the following examples. You should allow yourself approximately 5 minutes to complete these questions.

Passage 1:

Sarah, Mark and Jonathan are office workers at ABC Ltd. Time pressure increases the level of stress suffered by all ABC office workers, as does the shortening of coffee breaks. For all ABC office workers: if they suffer from increased levels of stress then their production rate will fall, working under time pressure impairs the quality of their work, and the shortening of coffee breaks reduces their commitment to ABC.

Question 14:

If Jonathan suffers from increased levels of stress then the quality of his work will fall.

       True   False   Maybe

Question 15:

If Sarah's commitment to ABC has been reduced but her production rate has increased, then her coffee break has not been reduced.

       True   False   Maybe

Question 16:

Mark has increased his production rate despite working under time pressure.

       True   False   Maybe

LOGICAL REASONING – TYPE B

These questions are designed to measure your ability to evaluate information carefully and identify logical connections. From a number of pieces of information (all of which are true), you have to identify those that are needed to solve a problem and record your answer by circling the appropriate numbers in answer boxes.

Try the following questions. You should allow yourself approximately 4 minutes to complete these questions.

Question 17:

A group of students have been asked to discover the code for the letter N. They do not know this code, but they do have the six pieces of information below. Assuming that they know letters in this code consist of different combinations of two distinct elements, dots and dashes, which THREE of these pieces of information do they need to give them the right answer?

1   A is the reverse of N.

2   A and X contain the same ratio of dots to dashes.

3   The two elements making N are the same and in the same order as the first two of the elements making X.

4   X is the opposite to P in that where P has dots, X has dashes and where P has dashes, X has dots.

5   Part of the element pattern in X is included in that of P.

6   P consists of one dot followed by two dashes and one dot.

Question 18:

Mr Lee has gone to the supermarket to buy one each of three different products for a neighbour who is ill. He knows that he has the exact money he needs but has forgotten to bring the shopping list with him. He also knows that the products his neighbour wants are included amongst the following: soap, shampoo, fuses, a light bulb, a bottle of bath oil and a packet of tea. Which TWO pieces of information does he need in order to decide which products to buy?

1   His neighbour wants at most two electrical and two toiletry items.

2   None of items mentioned above costs less than one quarter of his total money.

3   The soap only comes in packets of three.

4   Each toiletry item costs more than half his total money.

5   Tea is definitely one of the things he must buy.

6   His neighbour likes to read late into the night.

The example questions are supplied courtesy of Capita RAS, one of the UKs leading specialist consultancies.

Answers to Example Tests:

1. CBAD
2. CBDA
3. A (£78.10)
4. C (- £1.70)
5. D (£172.70)
6. B (17)
7. C (18)
8. E (24)
9. A (67)
10. D (18)
11. A (21)
12. B (19)
13. C (52)
14. Maybe
15. True
16. False
17. 3, 4, 6
18. 2, 4

Negotiating Salaries

PETER BRUNSWICK

Career Consultant

Salary negotiation is one of the most difficult and sensitive issues in employment. The first rule is *do not negotiate salary until you have been made an offer*. This is so important that it cannot be stressed enough.

One of the first questions any consultant will ask is, "What salary would you be looking for?" Don't be drawn. Ask them instead: "What salary does the job pay?" Alternatively try: "I would be interested in any offer you made", "What do you think the role is worth?" "I love the job and would seriously consider any offer which you made."

Tell them by all means what your salary is at the moment. Include all your bonuses, and if you are due for a rise shortly let them know. Discuss too those issues which will have a financial impact on your take home pay, but *do not tell them what salary you are looking for*. Until you have been offered the job, you are simply one more candidate. From the moment you give them a price you run the risk of not even being that. Only when they have made a firm offer to you are you in a position to negotiate a salary.

Rule number two: It is easier to negotiate a good hand badly than a bad hand well. Most people applying for jobs are not natural negotiators. Many candidates hate the whole concept. My advice then is don't negotiate. Just be open and honest and make sure that you are playing with a strong hand.

A strong hand only comes from having a choice, and choice is the result of well-organised hard work. Consider for a moment your position when you first start looking for a new job. The temptation is to only apply for those jobs which appear absolutely perfect. But applying for as many jobs as possible increases your chances of receiving more than one offer, resulting in the strength and freedom which a choice of jobs can deliver. With two offers on the table you don't need to bluff and counter bluff, to read up on negotiation techniques or worry about not getting a satisfactory offer. With a strong hand you can lay all your cards on the table, and enjoy the satisfaction of being scrupulously honest and up front with your prospective employer whilst still commanding the salary you want.

There can often be a timing issue with pulling in several job offers. Employers and agencies will push you to accept their offer while you still have outstanding interviews. This is a tricky situation to handle. Wherever possible you should be open and honest. When you have a difficulty or clash of interest *always* declare it and *always* ask for help in resolving it. For example:

"Dear sir, Thank you for your offer. I am very enthusiastic about both the job and the company and am keen to accept. Unfortunately I have a final interview with another employer on Tuesday and feel that I owe it to myself, my family and my prospective employer to attend it. I would be very

grateful if you could hold your offer open until then.
Please do not hesitate to call me if this is not
possible. Yours etc..."

While courtesy, honesty and professionalism are to be
striven for and will always be appreciated, you must make
sure you look after your own interests first. No one will ever
blame you for doing so. Take the following scenario as an
example:

"I'm sorry, but we are unable to hold the offer open
beyond noon today."

"In that case I will accept it"

"And your interview on Tuesday?"

"I've made the arrangements now and feel it would be
wrong of me to cancel at this late stage. But I am happy to
accept your job offer. When can I start?"

He knows and you know that your position has not moved
an inch. They have forced you to say what you did not want
to say. But you will still attend the other interview, and you
may well receive a more tempting offer. If you then turn the
first offer down, at least you can say you were entirely open
and honest. Candidates drop out of the running all the time.
You're not the first and you won't be the last. But what
happens if they turn up the pressure?

"I'm afraid that won't be good enough. Not only do we
need an acceptance but we need your assurance that you
will cancel all further interviews."

The more they push you to accept, the more they want
you. The ball is essentially in your court, and you shouldn't
allow yourself to be pressured into promises you don't wish
to make. Be particularly wary of agencies and consultants
pushing for acceptance. They often simply want to get you

onto their sales board before the close of the month. Make sure you are dealing directly with your prospective manager. If you feel uncomfortable about telling them you can't cancel a further interview, remember that they are only frightened that you'll be tempted away from their offer. In this situation, you're the one who's holding the reins. Be polite but firm, and keep in mind that it's *your* career in the balance.

Rule number three is that salary negotiation is not an us vs. them situation. The employer wants you to be happy with the offer, and they want to take you on board. Let them know that you are keen to accept. When you begin to discuss numbers, make the employer aware of your major financial commitments: childcare, that enormous mortgage you've recently taken on, payments on your new People Mover etc. They are much more likely to seriously consider requests that cover your tangible financial necessities than more trivial or intangible things. Commitments which indicate your maturity and responsibility are likely to be viewed more favourably as well. If you have any forthcoming rises due you in your present job, let your prospective employers know. You are looking for a competitive package, after all. Relocation is another expense which employers are usually willing to look at, though it's often a one-off payment. Your long-term career prospects can also be used as a bargaining tool: if you have a definite idea of the salary you want to (realistically) command in 5 years' time, you'll have a fairly good idea of what you are worth now.

You may think that once you have decided on satisfactory terms and figures it's time to leave the negotiating table. Not quite. Experienced negotiators will tell the employer at this point that they still believe, in the long term, that the job is worth more. Requesting a performance-related pay review in six months' time is often a satisfactory conclusion for everyone: you have the potential to increase your earnings within six months, and the employer knows you will be working exceptionally hard, both to prove yourself and to achieve the higher salary.

The techniques described are relatively simple, but there are many books which are entirely devoted to the art of negotiation. Mocking up on the subject will help you to get the most out of your next career move.

PETER BRUNSWICK *is a freelance career consultant.*

Salary Survey
STEVE FLATHER
The Reward Group

The people responsible for setting pay levels apply liberal quantities of art to a non-scientific subject. There is no such thing as the correct pay for a particular job. Wages, like many other aspects of society, are subject to a market economy. They are deternined by what organisations are prepared to pay for individuals of a given calibre and level of performance. This inevitably leads to the establishment of going rates., which are often specific to a conurbation or a region, and ultimately there are national and international market places.

In the setting of pay for, say, shop floor supervisors, a local labour market will be the benchmark, whereas for middle managers a regional market place would be more appropriate. For senior managers and directors a national or even international market place would be typical. The information contained within this article must, therefore, be applied to the specific circumstances of particular jobs.

SALARY SURVEY

The pay data provided in this chapter has been taken from R£WARD, The Management Salary Survey, published by The Reward Group. The data came from a large number of regional salary surveys undertaken by Reward across the whole of the UK. These surveys cover a wide range of jobs, but the focus for this article is on graduate pay, together with analysis by age.

The use of salary surveys is a skilled operation and the data that is contained in them, as illustrated in this article, needs to be understood and used appropriately. Those factors which predominantly affect a job's salary level need to be considered. We suggest that an appropriate way of using the data we are providing is for the reader to take a straight average of the information which is relevant to them.

The reader needs to take care in using the data that they understand the basis on which it has been collected and how it might then be used.

The data in this chapter has been collected only from employers and relates to individuals working within their organisations. However there is a further labour market relating to the recruitment market place. Typically, individuals will move from one job to another if the pay is sufficiently high to attract them to leave their job and move to another. There is an inevitable risk and insecurity associated with such a move and individuals require compensation for this, together with the usual rise in responsibility. The effect is to have a recruitment pay market which will be between 10 and 20% above the pay level for the equivalent level of job.

SALARY COMPARISONS

The information in the accompanying table relates purely to graduates. The age group is assumed to be in the 21-25 area unless otherwise stated by the participant. All Reward data is collected by job title and the data used in those tables therefore has been titled GRADUATE with a specialism as appropriate.

The table of Median basic pay level by discipline shows that in the latest survey the salaries offered to Engineering Graduates are currently the highest. This has not previously been the case for some years. Prior to this latest information, Research and Development and Scientific salaries were the highest. It therefore follows that, if this level for the Engineering salaries continues, there is a shortage of good Engineering Graduates which has driven up the salary. It may also be that Engineering Graduates are required, as the engineering element in Research and Development work increases as the demand for Manufacturing in its broadest sense continues.

The next highest level of pay of Graduates is for the Accounting function, followed by Personnel and interestingly Computing. In previous surveys the Computing salaries for both Graduates and those who have been employed for many years, have been the highest or nearly so.

The salary for Marketing Graduates follows and this has also slipped down the list slightly from previous years with the traditional Manufacturing functions of Production and Purchasing being next in line followed by Sales. There is something of a perversity in the salary levels for these latter

Pay Data:

Comparisons of Median Basic Salary - GRADUATES

Discipline	Median Basic Salary (£ p.a)
Engineering	17240
R & D/Scientific	17160
Accounts	16021
Personnel	15600
Computing	15555
Marketing	15455
Purchasing	15000
Sales	15000
Production	15000
Administration	12886
Upto 6 months Service	16000
6 to 12 months Service	16620
12 to 18 months Service	17257
18 to 24 months Service	17250

two functions which, in the Manufacturing industries, represent in many ways the wealth creation and selling processes. It is interesting to note that these functions, despite their pivotal nature to manufacturing, do not attract the highest salary.

In the case of the table of pay by Company Turnover, it will be noted that pay of Graduates is highest in companies with the largest turnover, that is over £500M per year. However, closer inspection of this list shows that, although it would be expected that the largest companies would pay the highest salaries, this is not the case for the next lower group of £200M to £500M which is seen to be next to the

Company Turnover	Median Basic Salary (£ p.a)
Up to £3M	16,459
£3M – £10M	16,000
£10M – £20M	**16,601**
£20M – £50M	16,000
£50M – £100M	16,793
£100M – £200M	15,000
£200M – £500M	15,045
Over £500M	17,500
Company Size (No. of Employees)	
Up to 100	17,060
101 to 200	16,485
201 to 500	16,480
501 to 1,000	15,228
1,001 to 4,000	16,011
4,001 to 10,000	—
Over 10,000	15,743
Regions of the UK	
South West	17,194
NorthWest	17,030
SouthEast	16,744
Scotland	16,698
London	16,488
West Midlands	16,254
North East	16,481
Eastern Counties	15,000
Northern Ireland	14,500
Progression of pay through age groups	
From 21-25 yrs old to 26-30 yrs old	+28%
From 26-30 yrs old to 31-35 yrs old	+20%
From 31-35 yrs old to 36-40 yrs old	+9%

bottom in the list in pay terms. Indeed, looking at the list as a whole it can be seen that there is virtually no relationship of the pay to the size of the organisation at Graduate levels. It is at Senior pay levels that this relationship becomes clear. This, in effect, illustrates the point that the Graduate pay market is very flat, set almost nationally and hardly related to the employing organisations.

The table showing pay by Company Size i.e. number of employees, is similarly perverse in its detail. In this particular case, the pay of Graduates in organisations of up to 100 employees is the highest and the pay of those in the largest organisations, over 10,000 employees, is the lowest. The pay level of those in the smallest companies is illustrative in so far as it is often the case that smaller companies, unburdened by substantial pay structures, are willing to pay the highest salaries to attract those whom they need to develop the organisation. Indeed in smaller organisations, each individual is a more substantial and integral part of the team and therefore attracting and retaining employees in this size of organisation is crucial. Therefore, smaller organisations tend to be more generous than the medium sized.

The table showing Regional Pay Levels once again illustrates that the pay market is driven by need rather than traditional pay structures. It would have been expected that the pay level for Graduates in the London area would be highest. In this table, however, it can be seen that the pay for Graduates is highest in the South West, with the North West taking the second position. Indeed, the next lowest is the South East with Scotland following hard on its heels and finally, London coming in the fifth or half way position. Once again this serves to illustrate that the pay market for Graduates is driven by specialisms rather than location. If there is a shortage of Graduates of a certain discipline within an area this will have the affect of driving up the pay. Clearly this is capricious and will move depending on the economy in each area. Attempting to forecast where the highest pay levels will be geographically would be a foolhardy exercise.

The table which shows the pay levels of Graduates with periods of employment serves to illustrate the well known phenomenon that pay levels for Graduates rise quickly in the early years and stabilise thereafter. In this particular case, the increase from the initial appointment to six months to the next level of six to twelve months is £600 and a similar increase to the next group of twelve to eighteen months. It then can be seen that the level is stable. This makes sense. After an initial training period, the pay of Graduates will become more aligned to that of others within the departments within which they work and, of course, the contribution that the Graduate makes to the organisation. This element of contribution increases as service and age rises and, as might be expected, the differentiators that are so crucial at the time of appointment change to being more related to the performance of the individual within the organisation. This point cannot be over stressed to Graduates.

CONCLUSIONS

This chapter has sought to illustrate the pay levels for graduates and related them to the pay for different disciplines, as well as factors such as size and region. Important features of graduates' pay include the tendency to be uniform across the UK in the early years, with differences occurring over time as performance levels and other regional industry or functional factors take over. What is clear is that pay rises rapidly for graduates in the early years and then plateau at the age of 35.

The Reward Group conducts salary surveys and analysis for many of the country's top companies. STEVE FLATHER is its Managing Director.

Overcoming the Experience Barrier

KATHRYN PUGH

Abbey National

Every company wants experience from its candidates and, almost by definition, every candidate applying will lack it. Nowhere is this more so than in the new graduate recruitment market.

The aim of this article is to help you identify what you have achieved so far. It will show you how to minimise your lack of experience and overcome this seemingly insurmountable problem which stands between you and your dream job.

The key to overcoming the experience barrier is to plan, prepare and take action. There are several easy and logical ways to help you do this: Firstly you need to think through all the life skills that you have acquired through school and university. Then you have to find a way of being seen to be the original person that you are in order to differentiate yourself from the competition. Thirdly you need to go and get the experience and finally you may need to re-evaluate your focus or apply for different types or levels of jobs. By the time you have read this article and taken action to follow some of the steps, you will be much more employable and you'll be ready to get the job you want.

The one thing to bear in mind throughout all of this is never to lie or over exaggerate your skills. You will not have done yourself any favours when you get caught out at interview. The best action, and the focus of this article, is to channel your creativity into not seeing your skills as a barrier at all, and to think positively.

The first tip is to list all the activities you have been involved in, in the last few years. This can be anything from playing sport, either as part of a team or as an individual, being secretary of a society, a committee member, being involved in putting together a play or exhibition, organising your own birthday party or an anniversary, visiting an elderly neighbour, planning your dissertation and university workload, baby sitting, doing a door-to-door collection for a charity, part-time work in a pub or shop, doing any hobby, running a marathon.

It is important to write everything down in a list, no matter how small or insignificant it may seem. The following is a list of commonly sought skills and attributes. There will almost certainly be others you can think of.

Effective Leadership	Commitment
Hard Work	Courage
Confidence	Teamwork
Intellectual Depth	Maturity
Judgement	Interpersonal skills

Once you have done this, identify the skills relevant for your business area and for each application and then match your experience to the skills required.

This will help you in two ways: it will give you examples of when you have demonstrated certain skills, but more importantly it will help you identify gaps in your experience that you can take action to resolve.

For example, if you have worked in a busy pub this demonstrates you can work in a team, that you can work under pressure, interact with customers, handle money and are prepared to work hard. If you have done any baby-sitting then you have been in a position of responsibility. Playing a team sport shows you are a team player. Individual sports can demonstrate commitment and dedication.

Most of us have done some of the activities above, so unless you have sat at home watching television you will have some experience and will have acquired some life skills. All the above can be used as evidence to demonstrate that you have the different skills and experience that employers require.

Secondly, applying for jobs is about competing, and as in any competitive field it helps if you are a unique product. In order to compete and succeed, make your experiences and skills interesting. Employers don't want to read fashionable buzz words or phrases, but do want to read something different. The key is to promote yourself, or what you are, in the best way possible. Promote yourself as a product and look on your application objectively. Only use relevant skills and pick up on any unusual aspects of your life skills.

The other important thing to do to win any competition is to play to your strengths. Although experience is important, it is not the only criteria a company is looking for in employees. Employers will always respond favourably to a positive application. Even if your only strengths are enthusiasm and dedication or knowledge of the company, demonstrate ways you have achieved or acquired these.

Once these steps have been completed you can identify gaps in your experiences and move to the third stage – getting the relevant experience. Try working for a few weeks in a related business area. Although it may be unpaid at a time when you may need to be getting cash to be able to survive financially, it is invariably time well spent and it will almost certainly pay off in the long term. It is surprising how much can be learnt in a fortnight and how much material it will give you to write on an application form or talk about in an interview. It demonstrates that you are committed to that business area and your career.

Experience can also be gained through joining a new society, helping out a charity for 2 hours a week, playing a new sport, starting an evening class or starting a part time job which uses different skills. Getting the right experience need not compromise your current job or interests.

And finally, if the barrier still seems insurmountable, change your focus and direction. Consider applying for jobs in a lower or related position. Get the experience and work your way up. If you graduated only a year or two ago, then consider starting afresh and apply for graduate positions and training schemes. Most companies understand that graduates don't have experience and next to the newly-qualified competition your experience will shine.

Although many graduates do lack experience and life skills, most simply fail to recognise the experience that they have. By following the steps outlined in this article it will become evident that graduates do have something interesting to offer a company.

Abbey National plc is the UK's 5th largest bank. KATHERYN PUGH *is a Corporate Affairs Manager*

Part Two

The Directory

Accountants > Agencies

A C M E Appointments . . . . www.acme-appts.co.uk
Accountancy Additions . . . . www.accountancyadditions.com
Accountancy Appointments . . . . www.accapp.co.uk
Accountancy Executive . . . . www.aea.co.uk
Accountancy Options . . . . www.accountancy-options.co.uk
Accountants on Call . . . . www.aocnet.com
Alexander Lloyd . . . . www.alexanderlloyd.co.uk
Badenoch & Clark . . . . www.badenochandclark.com
Cameron Kennedy Resources Ltd . . . . www.cameronkennedy.com
Finance Professionals. . . . . www.financeprofessions.com
Hays Accountancy Personnel . . . . www.hays-ap.com
Jonathan Wren & Co Ltd . . . . www.jwren.com
PSD Financial Services Recruitment . . . . www.psdgroup.com
Robert Half. . . . . www.roberthalf.net
Witan Jardine Financial Recruitment . . . . . . www.witanjardine.co.uk
Zenith Accountancy Ltd. . . . . www.zenithaccountancy.co.uk

Accountants > Firms

Arram Brlyn Gardner

www.abggroup.co.uk

We are a London based medium sized practice dedicated to the provision of a responsive and quality personal service second to none.

WWW.CHOICESONLINE.COM

AGN Shipleys. . . . . www.agnshipleys.com
Arram Brlyn Gardner . . . . www.abggroup.co.uk
Arthur Andersen. . . . . www.arthurandersen.com/ukcareers
Audit Commission. . . . . www.audit-commission.gov.uk

Audit Commission

www.audit-commission.gov.uk

The Audit Commission is an independent body responsible for ensuring that public money is used economically, efficiently and effectively.

WWW.CHOICESONLINE.COM

Baker Tilly . . . . www.bakertilly.co.uk
Barnes Roffe . . . . www.barnes-roffe.co.uk
BDO Stoy Hayward . . . . www.bdo.co.uk

Baker Tilly

www.bakertilly.co.uk

2 Bloomsbury Street, London, WC1B 3ST
t: 020 7413 5432

Baker Tilly is a Top 10 firm of accountants and business advisers in the UK - and one of the fastest growing. Forward looking and entrepreneurial, we've developed a very distinctive brand of professional but highly personal service. Vacancies exist for 50+ graduates annually in audit, tax, business recovery and corporate finance. You will find us a 'genuinely different firm'.

WWW.CHOICESONLINE.COM

Bentley Jennison . . . . www.bentley-jennison.co.uk
BKR Haines Watts . . . . www.hwca.com
Blick Rothenberg . . . . www.blickrothenberg.com
Brebner Allen and Trapp . . . . www.brebner.co.uk
Bright Grahame Murray . . . . www.bgm.co.uk
Burnett Swayne . . . . www.burnettswayne.co.uk
Buzzacott . . . . www.buzzacott.co.uk

Barnes Roffe

www.barnes-roffe.co.uk

Leyton, Holborn, Dartford, Mayfair and Uxbridge

Brebner Allen and Trapp

www.brebner.co.uk

The Quadrangle, 180 Wardour Street, London, W1F 8LB
t: 020 7734 2244

With international connections through ICC, BAT is a medium sized firm of chartered accountants.

Casson Beckman . . . . www.cassonbeckman.co.uk
Chantrey Vellacott . . . . www.cvdfk.com
Clyde & Co . . . . www.clydeco.com

District Audit

www.district-audit.gov.uk

Unique, complex and stimulating - the work of District Audit can be described in many ways. The fact is, few organisations can match the variety or scope of activities we undertake. As the audit arm of the Audit Commission (www.audit-commission.gov.uk), we're responsible for ensuring that £100 billion of public money is wisely spent by local authorities and the health service.

Ernst & Young

www.ey.com/uk/graduate
grad.rec@cc.ernsty.co.uk

Burnett Swayne

www.burnettswayne.co.uk

Charter Court, 3rd Avenue, Southampton,
t: 023 8070 2345 **f:** 023 8070 2570

N of vacancies: We require 3/4 graduates to join our team of experienced and professional staff.

Application procedure: Apply in writing to Roy Longman at the above address enclosing an up to date CV.

Opportunities available: All successful applicants will be trained according to a student contract in a wide variety of work, leading to ICAEW qualification.

Business description: Burnett Swayne is a highly successful chartered accountants and is one of the largest practices in the south.

Disciplines: If you are an enthusiastic and committed individual, looking for a challenging role, then we would be interested in hearing from you.

WWW.CHOICESONLINE.COM

Cooper-Parry

COOPER·PARRY

www.cooperparry.com
SarahL@cooperparry.com

102 Friar Gate, Derby, DE1 1FH
t: 01332 295 544

Business Description:
Cooper Parry is a leading firm of Chartered Accountants led by 24 partners, employing over 200 staff. With a reputation for quality we serve a variety of clients in the owner-managed business sector.

A member of the International Group of Accounting Firms, we have contacts in most of the world's financial centres. From our Derby and Nottingham offices, we provide diverse services to industry, commerce and the professions including corporate/management advice, audit, accountancy and taxation. In addition we offer IT Consultancy and specialist advice on business recovery and insolvency.

No of Vacancies
6-8

Opportunities Available:
We offer a three year training programme designed to enhance your personal skills and knowledge through our internal modular development programmes and through self-learning.

Disciplines:
We accept graduates from all disciplines although it is essential that you have or expect to gain a 2:1 honours degree.

Application Procedure:
By contacting Sarah Loates on 01332 295544 or e-mail her at SarahL@cooperparry.com application forms are also available on-line at www.cooperparry.com

Dixon Wilson

DIXON WILSON
CHARTERED ACCOUNTANTS

www.dixonwilson.com

PO Box 900, Rotherwick House,
3 Thomas More Street,
London, E1W 9YX
t: 020 7628 4321 **f:** 020 7702 9769

Dixon Wilson is a leading firm of Chartered Accountants with offices in London and Paris. With a professional team of just over 100 we have intentionally remained independent and relatively small in order to provide a very personal service.

Graduate recruitment
We take on up to 16 graduates each year with intakes beginning in March and September. We also accept 2-3 trainees for our Paris office.

Training
We have an "end-loaded" training programme where our trainees prepare for exams with a leading firm of commercial tutors, Financial Training, who provide a comprehensive programme. This is enhanced by in-house training sessions and a further intensive course before examinations.

Requirements
Applicants should have 24 UCAS points and a 2:1 degree. A good pass in A-level Maths is advantageous.

Apply
An application form can be downloaded from the website and should be sent to the Staff Manager at the above address.

haysmacintyre . . . . www.haysmacintyre.com
HLB Kidsons. . . . . www.hlbkidsons.co.uk
Horwath Clark Whitehill . . . . www.horwathcw.co.uk

HAT Group of Accountants

www.hatgroup.co.uk
recruit@hatgroup.co.uk

12 Cock Lane, London, EC1A 9BU
t: 020 7213 9911 **f:** 020 7213 9922

HAT is a training consortium with 30 member firms of accountants, based primarily in London and the South East. We recruit trainee Chartered Accountants on their behalf

KPMG

www.kpmgcareers.co.uk

Graduate Recruitment Department,
1 Puddle Dock, London, EC4V 3PD
t: 0500 664 665

If you aspire to be the best, we've already got one thing in common. We are the largest professional firm of business advisors in Europe, and one of the largest in the world. We offer a stimulating working environment working with our wide portfolio of clients.

Jacksons . . . . www.jacksonsgroup.com
James & Cowper . . . . www.jamescowper.co.uk

Lee & Allen Consulting plc

www.lee-and-allen.com

Hulton House, 166 Fleet Street, London, EC4A 2DY
t: 020 7353 5550

Lee and Allen is a City based independent team of forensic Accountants.

Lubbock Fine

www.lubbockfine.co.uk

Russell Bedford House, City Forum,
250 City Road, London, EC1V 2QQ
t: 020 7490 7766

JobServe	www.accountancy.jobserve.com
Johnston Carmichael	www.jcca.co.uk
Kingston Smith	www.kingstonsmith.co.uk
KPMG	www.kpmgcareers.co.uk
Larking Gowen	www.larkinggowen.co.uk
Lee & Allen Consulting plc	www.lee-and-allen.com
Levy Gee	www.levygee.com
Littlejohn Frazer	www.littlejohnfrazer.com
Lubbock Fine	www.lubbockfine.co.uk
MacIntyre Hudson	www.macintyrehudson.co.uk

PricewaterhouseCoopers

www.pwcglobal.com/uk/graduate_careers/

Get ready. Your perfect career starts here.

If you're after the best training, the best prospects and the best business culture, you're looking at the right firm. We set the career standards in assurance, tax and legal, risk management, financial consulting, IT, e-business and actuarial, so come and see where you fit in at PricewaterhouseCoopers. We also offer a range of student and undergraduate programmes - to find out more visit www.pwcglobal.com/uk/sidp/

MacIntyre Hudson

MACINTYRE HUDSON
GROUP OF COMPANIES

www.macintrehudson.co.uk

dianawalker@macintyrehudson.co.uk

Moorgate House, 201 Silbury Boulevard,
Milton Keynes, MK9 1LZ
t: 01908 662255

N of vacancies: 30 Any degree discipline is suitable

Locations: Bedford, Central London, North London, Chelmsford, High Wycombe, Leicester, Milton Keynes, Northampton, Peterborough

MacIntyre Hudson are a well established firm of chartered accountants, with more than a 100 years experience behind them. They offer clients a unique range of skills and knowledge that go beyond those of traditional chartered accountants. MacIntyre Hudson firmly believe that accountancy is not just about numbers, it is about people.

Newby Castleman

www.newbycastleman.co.uk

Newby Castleman is one of the largest independent firms of chartered accountants in the East Midlands.

Mazars Neville Russell . . . . www.mazars-nr.co.uk

Pirdie:Brewster

www.pirdie-brewster.com

PKF

www.pkf.co.uk

New Garden House, 78 Hatton Garden, London, EC1N 8JA
t: 020 7831 7393 **f:** 020 7782 9430

PKF is a national firm of chartered accountants and business advisors, with over 25 regional offices throughout the UK. PKF International employs 8,000 staff worldwide with a presence in most major cities around the globe.

Principle services
Assurance & Advisory, Consultancy, Corporate Finance, Corporate Recovery & Insolvency, Forensic and Taxation.

Opportunities available
65 vacancies annually in the UK for graduates to undertake the ACA qualification. The growth of international business has meant that many staff have the opportunity to work overseas after qualification.

Further information
Visit the website for further details of graduate opportunities.

Mazars Neville Russell

www.mazars-nr.co.uk

24 Bevis Marks, London, EC3A 7NR
t: 020 7377 1000 **f:** 020 7377 8931

Vacancies available in the following offices: Brighton, Bristol, Dudley, Huddersfield, Ilford, London, Luton, Milton Keynes, Nottingham, Poole, Stockport and Sutton.

Mazars Neville Russell is a leading UK accountancy firm and is part of an international firm represented in 44 counties worldwide.

Moore Stephens

MOORE STEPHENS
CHARTERED ACCOUNTANTS

www.moorestephens.com
david.chopping@@moorestephens.com
St Paul's House, Warwick Lane, London, EC4P 4BN
t: 020 7334 9191

Disciplines involved: Any 2:1 honours degree or above.

No. of vacancies: Approx.40

Application procedure: For further details, you should obtain a copy of our graduate recruitment brochure from your careers advisory service

Moore Stephens International Limited is one of the worlds leading accounting and consulting networks with 352 offices in 78 countries.

Rees Pollock

www.reespollock.co.uk

7 Pilgrim Street, London, EC4V 6DR
t: 020 7329 6404

Discipline Required: Any degree but minimum 26 UCAS points

Contact: Catherine Kimberlin, Staff Partner.

Small firm of chartered accountants who left Ernst and Young in 1990 to specialise in small and medium companies. Range of work experience including audits, investigation, litigation support and general business advice.

Rawlinson & Hunter

RAWLINSON & HUNTER

www.rawlinson-hunter.com

Eagle House, 110 Jermyn Street, London, SW1Y 6RH
t: 020 7451 9000

Graduate requirement: We recruit talented graduates and established professionals who are looking for a challenging career and a demanding client portfolio. We are looking for people who will progress through the firm. Our view is long term: we are looking for future partners.

Training: Our individually tailored training programmes offer study support to take you exactly where you want to go. Of course, as professional advisers, you need more than just knowledge of finance . So we also provide training in personal development, management and IT skills.

Locations: Our head office and the centre of our international network is the UK firm. We have two offices, in St James and in Ewell, Surrey.

Rawlinson & Hunter is an international firm of chartered accountants, specialising in financial advice and taxation. Our network of offices stretches from our headquarters in London to Sydney, Australia, through Switzerland and the Channel Islands, Bermuda and the Caribbean.

Menzies Ltd . . . . www.menzies.co.uk
Mercer & Hole . . . . www.mercerhole.co.uk
Moore Stephens . . . . www.moorestephens.com
Morgan Brown Spofforth . . . . www.morgangroup.co.uk
Morley & Scott . . . . www.morley-scott.co.uk
Newby Castleman . . . . www.newbycastleman.co.uk
Pirdie:Brewster . . . . www.pirdie-brewster.com

Saffery Champness

Saffery Champness
CHARTERED ACCOUNTANTS

www.saffery.com

Fairfax House, Fulwood Place, Gray's Inn, London, WC1V 6UB

t: 020 7405 2828 **f:** 020 7405 7887

Saffery Champness is a leading firm of chartered accountants, one of the top twenty in the UK.

While our work is very general, we also operate in a number of niche market sectors, primarily agriculture and estate but with growing practices in the charities and entertainment sectors.

We are IIP registered and offer excellent development and training programmes.

For full details of graduate opportunities please visit our web site at www.saffery.com

WWW.CHOICESONLINE.COM

PKF . . . . www.pkf.co.uk
Price Bailey . . . . www.pricebailey.co.uk
PricewaterhouseCoopers www.pwcglobal.com/uk/graduate_careers/
PricewaterhouseCoopers www.pwcglobal.com/uk/graduate_careers/
Rawlinson & Hunter . . . . www.rawlinson-hunter.com
Rees Pollock . . . . www.reespollock.co.uk
Reeves & Neylan . . . . www.reeves&neylan.co.uk
RSM Robson Rhodes . . . . www.rsmi.co.uk
Saffery Champness . . . . www.saffery.com
Scott-Moncrieff . . . . www.scott-moncrieff.co.uk
Smith & Williamson . . . . www.smith.williamson.co.uk
Tenon Group . . . . www.tenongroup.com

Smith & Williamson

Smith & Williamson

www.smith.williamson.co.uk
Personnel@smith.williamson.co.uk

1 Riding House Street, London, W1A 3AS
t: 020 7637 5377

We are recruiting to our London, North London, Guildford and Salisbury offices.

Disciplines involved: Grade C or above in GCSE Mathematics and English. Minimum 22 UCAS points (excluding general studies). 2.1 degree (any discipline).

Types of work offered: Audit and business services; investment management; corporate tax; private tax.

N of vacancies: Audit and Business Services (16); Investment Management (2); Corporate Tax (6); Personal Tax and Trusts (6); Pensions and Financial Planning (2), Corporate Recovery (2).

Application procedure: Application form and graduate brochure available online.

Smith & Williamson are one of the leading chartered accountancy firms. They are a provider of investment management, financial advisory and accountancy services to private clients, smaller and medium sized companies and professional partnerships.

Accountants > Institutes & Media

Association of Chartered Certified Accountants

www.accaglobal.com

29 Lincoln's Inn Fields, London, WC2A 3EE
t: 020 7396 5800 **f:** 020 7396 5858

The Association of Chartered Certified Accountants (ACCA)has been recognised and respected across the world for almost 100 years, and currently has nearly 300,000 students and members in 160 countries.

The ACCA qualification is a highly relevant, targeted combination of study and practical experience, and is widely recognised in all sectors throughout the world.

The Association of Corporate Treasurers

www.treasurers.org

Ocean House, 10/12 Little Trinity Lane, London, EC4V 2DJ
t: 0207 213 9728 **f:** 020 7248 2591

The Association of Corporate Treasurers is the UK's only professional body to offer specialised qualifications in treasury, risk and international cash management. Membership is available at 3 levels via examination.

A range of conferences and a monthly journal, The Treasurer, promote best practice in treasury.

The Association has approximately 500 Fellows, 1400 Members, 1200 Associate Members and more than 1150 professionals enrolled on examination courses.

Association of Chartered Certified Accountants . . . .
. . . . www.accaglobal.com
Chartered Institute of Management Accountants . . www.cima.org.uk
Chartered Institute of Taxation . . . . www.tax.org.uk
Institute of Chartered Accountants in England & Wales . . . .
. . . . www.icaew.co.uk
Institute of Company Accountants 0117 973 8261
Institute of Financial Accountants . . . . www.ifa.org.uk
The Association of Corporate Treasurers . . . www.treasurers.org

---

The Institute of Chartered Accountants of Scotland

www.icas.org.uk

CA House, 21 Haymarket Yards, Edinburgh, EH12 5BH
t: 0131 347 0161 **f:** 0131 349 0108

The Institute of Chartered Accountants of Scotland (ICAS) received its Royal Charter in 1854 and is the oldest professional body of accountants in the world. It was the first to adopt the designation "Chartered Accountant" and the designatory letters "CA" are still an exclusive privilege in the UK for members of the Scottish Institute.

The Institute of Chartered Accountants of Scotland . . . .
. . . . www.icas.org.uk

Actuaries > Agencies

Darwin Rhodes . . . . www.darwinrhodes.co.uk
GAAPS Ltd. . . . . www.gaaps.co.uk
Hanover Search & Selection . . . . www.hanover-search.com

GAAPS Ltd.

www.gaaps.co.uk

Grafton House, 2-3 Golden Square, London, W1R 3AD
t: 020 7437 8899 **f:** 020 7437 8699

Actuaries > Employers > Firms

Andersen........................... www.arthurandersen.co.uk
Aon Consulting .... www.aon.co.uk
Bacon & Woodrow.................. www.bacon-woodrow.com
Barnett Waddingham .... www.barnett-waddingham.co.uk
Black Mountain International Ltd ..... www.blackmountainmgt.com
Buck Consultants .... www.buckconsultants.co.uk

Milliman UK

www.millimanuk.com
jill_poole@millimanuk.com

Finsbury Tower, 103-105 Bunhill Row, London, EC1Y 8LZ
t: 020 78476100

Milliman UK is a rapidly expanding actuarial consultancy which is part of Milliman Global, a leading international consulting organisation to the insurance industry. We offer students the opportunity to gain experience in both life and general insurance. We are recruiting for up to 4 honours graduates with good mathematical skills. Generous study leave is provided and tuition costs are paid.

Please apply with a standard application form to Jill Poole, London HR Manager.

Aon Consulting

www.aon.co.uk

No of vacancies: 30 - 35 Consulting vacancies nationwide.16 - 20 Risk and General Management vacancies mainly in London

Subjects of study: For Consulting 2i or higher in a numerate discipline. For Risk and General Management 2ii or higher in any discipline.

Training & development Structured training programme towards relevant qualifications.

Vacation placements: We offer 8 week summer placements for those wishing to be Consultant Actuaries.

Introduction
Aon Limited is a dominant player in the risk management, reinsurance broking, actuarial and employee benefits consultancy business.

We have opportunities for graduates from a variety of backgrounds and offer two distinct training programmes for actuarial consultants and risk management professionals and general managers.

Consulting
Aon Consulting is one of the largest actuarial employee benefit and human resources consultancies in the UK, with over 1500 staff in 16 locations. One of the largest areas of activity is corporate pensions consulting.

Risk and General Management
Aon Limited is the leading retail insurance and risk management provider in the UK. Our mission is to find solutions, whether insurance or reinsurance. You would rotate through a number of placements in different parts of the business throughout the 18-month training period.

Applications by 31 December 2001 on Employers Application Form. Completed application forms should be sent to Graduate Recruitment Co-ordinator, Aon LTD, 8 Devonshire Square, London, EC2M 4PL

Hymans Robertson

 Hymans Robertson

www.hymans.co.uk
recruitment@hymans.co.uk

Finsbury Tower, 103-105 Bunhill Row, London, EC1Y 8LZ.
Tel: 020 7847 6000
221 West George Street, Glasgow, G2 2ND.
Tel: 0141 248 7007

An expanding independent actuarial consultancy, which offers students the opportunity to gain experience in employee benefits and pensions. Recruits up to 8 good quality graduates in mathematics, statistics, or economics. Generous study leave given and tuition costs paid.

Standard Application Form to Jill Poole, London HR Manager, or Karen McGrath, Human Resources Department, Glasgow.

Callund Consulting . . . . www.callund.com
Dundas & Wilson . . . . www.arthurendersen.com
English Matthews Brockman . . . . www.emb.co.uk
Entergia Limited . . . . www.entergialtd .co.uk
Ernst & Young . . . . www.ey.com/uk
Garvin & Co . . . . www.garvinco.com

Buck Consultants

www.buckconsultants.co.uk

Buck Consultants is a firm of employee benefit consultants and actuaries operating through 65 offices in 17 countries around the world. In the UK we have over 25 years' experience advising on all aspects of the provision and implementation of employee benefits for staff in corporations, local government departments and non-profit making institutions.

Towers Perrin/Tillinghast

Towers Perrin

BUILDING RELATIONSHIPS ■ PRODUCING RESULTS™

www.towers.com

Castlewood House, 77 91 New Oxford Street,
London, WC1A 1PX **t:** 020 7379 4411

Towers Perrin is one of the largest employers of actuaries in the UK. It is an international firm wholly owned by its senior employees.

Offices
A global company with over 8,500 employees in over 23 countries across the UK, Australia, Canada, Europe, Latin America and the United States.

Training
Is both formal and on the job. Graduates will study towards their actuarial examinations.

Requirements
Applicants should have 3 high A level results, including a B in Mathematics and be expecting a minimum of a 2:1 in any numerate or scientific discipline honours degree.

How to apply
Check the with your careers service to see if Towers Perrin are visiting your university campus. Otherwise call 020 8895 3855 or email act_grads@towers.com for an application form and brochure.

Bacon & Woodrow

www.bacon-woodrow.com

Bacon & Woodrow is one of the UK's leading firm of actuaries and consultants and a member of Woodrow Milliman, the international network of actuarial and consulting firms.

William M Mercer Ltd

www.wmmercer.com/ukgrads
graduates@uk.wmmercer.com

Jo Mitchell, Westgate House,
52 Westgate, Chichester, PO19 3HF
t: 01243 522 707

Business Description:
William M Mercer Ltd is a world leader in the field of acturial, employee benefits and human resources consultancy.

No of Vacancies:
We have a number of vacancies for graduates with a minimum 24 UCAS points and 2.1 degree in a business or numerate-related subject.

Opportunities Available:
Approximately 90 challenging career opportunities exist within our acturial, HR, International and Investment Consulting practices.

Application Procedure:
Please send an employer or standard application form to the above address. Alternatively, on-line application forms are available at www.wmmercer.com/ukgrads

Gissings Consultancy Services . . . . wwwgissings.co.uk
Government Actuarys Department . . . . www.gad.gov.uk
HSBC Actuaries and Consultants Ltd . . . .
 . . . . www.actuariesandconsultants.hsbc.co.uk
Hymans Robertson . . . . www.hymans.co.uk
KPMG . . . . www.kpmgcareers.co.uk
Lane, Clark and Peacock . . . . www.lcp-actuaries.co.uk
Mercer & Hole . . . . www.mercerhole.co.uk
Milliman UK . . . . www.millimanuk.com

Nigel Sloam & Co. www.nigelsloam.co.uk
Punter Southall & Company Ltd . . . . www.puntersouthall.com
Towers Perrin/Tillinghast. . . . . www.towers.com
Watson Wyatt Worldwide . . . . www.watsonwyatt.com/graduate
William M Mercer Ltd . . . . www.wmmercer.com/ukgrads
Windsor Life Assurance. . . . . www.windsorlifeassurance.co.uk

Actuaries > Employers > Insurance Companies

AMP UK plc . . . . www.amp.co.uk
AXA Group . . . . www.axa.co.uk
Barclays Life Assurance Company Ltd . . . . www.life.barclays.co.uk
Brittanic Assurance Plc . . . . www.brittanicassurance.co.uk
Canada Life Ltd. . . . . www.canadalife.co.uk
Clerical Medical . . . . www.clericalmedical.co.uk
Co-operative Insurance Society Ltd . . . . www.cis.co.uk
Countrywide Assured . . . . www.countrywideassured.co.uk
Eagle Star Life Assurance Ltd . . . . www.eaglestardirect.co.uk
Friends Provident. . . . . www.friendsprovident.co.uk
Guardian Financial Services. . . . . www.guardianfs.co.uk
Halifax plc . . . . www.halifax.co.uk
HSBC . . . . www.hsbc.com/recruitment
Legal & General Assurance plc . . . . . . www.legal-and-general.co.uk

Co-operative Insurance Society Ltd

www.cis.co.uk

CIS is a leading nationwide insurer with over 130 years' experience and a customer base in excess of 3 million. Throughout the UK we have around 4,000 representatives offering professional advice in customers' homes, tailored to their individual requirements.

AXA Group

AXA UK   AXA Insurance   AXA Sun Life

107 Cheapside, London, EC2V 6DU

Types of vacancies: Managerial, Sales, Operations, Actuarial. Additional vacancies may occur during the year.

Minimum requirement: 22 UCAS points plus a minimum 2:2, Actuarial candidates need a 2:1 plus sufficient qualifications to join the Institute of Actuaries.

Application procedure: Send a detailed CV with covering letter to Tricia King, Graduate Manager, AXA UK at the above address. Please ensure you give full details of your A level/Highers - or equivalent - subjects and results.

A Global Financial Business

We are a financial services business, focused on insurance and related products. The Group is the 15th largest company in the World.

Following major acquisitions in the UK we have just completed a successful integration programme. There are now tremendous opportunities for the right people to build on the integration and take us through to a new era.

Two Management Training Schemes

We currently have two management training schemes. One through AXA Insurance and the other through AXA Sun Life offering placements throughout the respective businesses, with the flexibility to tailor these to your strengths and interests. Central and local training ensure that all our graduates achieve the central scheme objectives as well as locally agreed ones. All graduates attend the European Graduates Forum at one of our training centres in Southern France. Graduate Management Trainees are expected to pass professional exams in a relevant area.

AXA Group Continued

Although there are some opportunities in other offices if preferred, AXA Insurance vacancies are mainly based in London and AXA Sun Life vacancies in Bristol.

Comprehensive management development
Both schemes last about 2 years although our comprehensive management development programme ensures that you will be developing your skills throughout your career. Non scheme vacancies also offer full training and career management and are based throughout the UK. As your career develops global opportunities will become available.

Team workers wanted
We are looking for good team workers who are prepared to take the lead, people with ambition and determination who really want to make a difference and won't balk at hard work. We want to continue to grow and we need the right people to make that happen.

Lloyds TSB plc . . . . www.lloydstsb.co.uk
MGM Assurance . . . . www.mgmassurance.co.uk
National Mutual Life Assurance Society . . . .
. . . . www.nationalmutual.co.uk
NFU Mutual . . . . www.nfumutual.co.uk

Scottish Amicable Life plc

www.scottishamicable.co.uk

PO Box 25, Craigforth, Stirling, FK9 4UE
t: 01786 448 844

Since 1997, Scottish Amicable has been part of the Prudential group, one of the UK's largest financial services providers with total funds under management of over £156 billion as at 31 December 2000.

Scottish Amicable is based in Stirling.

Scottish Equitable plc

www.scottishequitable.co.uk

Edinburgh Park, Edinburgh, EH12 9SE

t: 0131 339 9191

As one of the UK's leading pension and personal investment product providers, we offer our employees excellent rewards, including the potential for career progression.

Scottish Equitable is based in Edinburgh.

Standard Life Assurance Company

STANDARD LIFE®

www.individuals.co.uk

Standard life House, 30 Lothian Road, Edinburgh, EH1 2DH

t: 0131 225 2552 **f:** 0131 245 0520

Business description: Standard Life currently has over Eu78 billion assets under management. What this means is that we currently have more assets under management than the market value of Boots, Tesco, Marks & Spencer and British airways combined. Having been providing financial services since 1825, it follows that we have got a good deal of experience to work from.

No of vacancies: We have a numbered of vacancies for qualified graduates.

Opportunities available: Opportunities are available such as training schemes and competitive salaries.

Application procedure: application forms are available on-line at the web-site address below.

More information can be found on-line at: www.individuals.co.uk

Norwich Union plc . . . . www.norwichunion.co.uk
Pinnacle Assurance . . . . www.pinnacle.co.uk
Prudential Corporation plc . . . . www.prudential.co.uk
Royal Liver . . . . www.royal-liver.com
Scottish Amicable Life plc . . . . www.scottishamicable.co.uk
Scottish Equitable plc . . . . www.scottishequitable.co.uk
Scottish Widows . . . . www.scottishwidows.co.uk
Skandia Life Assurance . . . . www.skandia.co.uk
Standard Life Assurance Company . . . . . . www.individuals.co.uk
Swiss Life (UK) plc . . . . www.swisslife.co.uk
Swiss Re . . . . www.swissre.com
Zurich Financial Services . . . . www.zurich.co.uk

Actuaries > Insitutes & Media

Actuary, The . . . . www.actuaries.org.uk
Institute of Actuaries . . . . www.actuaries.org.uk
Proactivity . . . . www.proactivity.net

Advertising & Marketing > BusinessPress

Broadcast . . . . www.produxion.com
Campaign . . . . www.campaignlive.com
Marketing . . . . www.marketing.haynet.com
Marketing Direct . . . . www.mxdirect.co.uk
Marketing Week . . . . www.marketing-week.co.uk
PR Week . . . . www.prweekuk.com
Precision Marketing . . . . www.mad.co.uk
Professional Marketing . . . . www.pmint.co.uk

Advertising & Marketing > Employers

Abbott Mead Vickers BBDO . . . . www.amvbbdo.com

Abbott Mead Vickers BBDO

www.amvbbdo.com

Why consider us
We create something, so there is satisfaction. We do it as a team, so there is friendship and we do something useful, so there is a sense of purpose.

Good luck with your application and thank you for considering Abbott Mead Vickers.BBDO.

David Abbott

ABBOTT MEAD VICKERS.BBDO

Bartle Bogle Hegarty Ltd

www.bartleboglehegarty.com

We were founded in 1982 and 19 years later, we still work with our three founding clients - Audi, Interbrew and Levi's. We now have 30 clients including Lynx, Impulse, One 2 One and Barclays, to name a few.

BBH has billings of £550 million worldwide and offices in London, New York and Singapore.

Brann Worldwide

www.brann.com

Brann Worldwide is one of the largest direct marketing organisations in the world.

BMP DDB

www.bmpddb.com
graduates@bmpddb.com

"..you would have to look to the world of football - and draw parallels with Manchester United - to understand just how total the domination of BMP DDB has been in the world of Advertising."

Evening Standard

Banks Hoggins O'Shea / FCB . . . . www.fcb.com
Bartle Bogle Hegarty Ltd . . . . www.bartleboglehegarty.com
Bates UK . . . . www.batesuk.com
BMP DDB . . . . www.bmpddb.com
Brann Worldwide . . . . www.brann.com
CDP Travies sully . . . . www.cdp-travissully.com
DArcy . . . . www.darcyww.com

D'Arcy

www.darcyww.com

123 Buckingham Palace Road, London, SW1W 9D2
t: 020 77511800

D'Arcy, one of the world's largest global communications companies, is part of The Bcom3 Group. We have more than 6,000 employees in 131 offices in 75 countries. Our major worldwide clients include Procter & Gamble, General Motors, Fiat, M&M Mars, The Coca-Cola Company, Burger King, Philips and Ernst & Young. Make your mark at D'Arcy.

Euro RSCG Wnek Gosper

www.eurorscg.co.uk

11 Great Newport Street, London, WC2H 7JA

"The coolest company to work for." - The Guardian

Euro RSCG Wnek Gosper. . . . . www.eurorscg.co.uk

QAS

www.qas.com

George West House, 2 - 3 Clapham Common North Side, London, SW4 0QL

Rapid career development makes QAS the perfect place for ambitious IT, sales and marketing professionals.

J Walter Thompson

J Walter Thompson

www.jwtworld.com

40 Berkeley Square, London, W1X 6AD
t: 020 7499 4040

J Walter Thompson, the world's first advertising agency, iis transforming into the world's first global brand communications company, with clients such as Nike, Siemens and Merrill Lynch.

It currently has over 250 offices and affiliates covering 88 countries and employing over 9,200 people.

UK offices in London and Manchester. Apply directly to relevant office.

List-Link International

www.list-link.com

List-Link International is the main portal to the direct marketing industry.

Grey Worldwide . . . . www.grey.com
HHCL . . . . www.hhcl.com
J Walter Thompson . . . . www.jwtworld.com
Leagas Delaney . . . . www.leagasdelaney.com
Leo Burnett Ltd . . . . www.leoburnett.com
List-Link International . . . . www.list-link.com
Lowe Lintas . . . . www.lowelintas.co.uk
M & C Saatchi . . . . www.mcsaatchi.com

Ogilvy

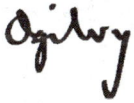

www.Ogilvy.com

10 Cabot Square, Canary Wharf, London, E14 4QB
t: 020 7345 3000

Disciplines involved: No specific degree requirements.

Salary: £16,000 - £18,000 BUPA life insurance Subsided gym membership.

Graduate Recruitment Brochure available. To request write to the Graduate Recruitment Manager at the above address

Ogilvy in London is one of the leading offices in Ogilvy Worldwide. These companies share a remarkable common culture with 359 other Ogilvy offices in 100 countries, hence comprising one of the world's largest agency networks, employing over 8,500 people in over 70 languages.

WPP Group

www.wpp.com

27 Farm Street, London, W1J 5RJ
t: 020 7408 2204 **f:** 020 7493 6819

Service sectors: Advertising, media investment management, information and consultancy, public relations and public affairs, branding and identity, healthcare and specialist communications.

WPP is one of the worlds leading communications services groups, providing services to local, multinational and global clients, including more than 300 of the Fortune Global 500. Our 65,000 people work out of 1300 offices in 92 countries.

Application form available from www.wpp.com

Deadline for entry 7th December 2001

WWW.CHOICESONLINE.COM

McCann Erickson . . . . www.mccann.com
Ogilvy . . . . www.Ogilvy.com
Publicis Ltd . . . . www.publicis.co.uk
QAS . . . . www.qas.com
Rainey Kelly Campbell Roalfe/Y&R . . . . www.yr.com
Research International . . . . www.research-int.com
Saatchi & Saatchi plc . . . . www.saatchi-saatchi.com
TBWA . . . . www.tbwa.co.uk
The Marketing Store Worldwide . . . . www.tmsw.co.uk
WCRS . . . . www.wcrs.com
WPP Group . . . . www.wpp.com

Architecture

Architecture and Surveying Institute

www.asi.org.uk
mail@asi.org.uk

St Mary House, 15 St Mary Street,
Chippenham, SN15 3WD
t: 01249 444 505 **f:** 01249 443 602

A multi-disciplinary Institute serving the construction industry.

Building Design Partnership

www.bdp.co.uk

Po Box 4WD, 16 Gresse Street,
London, W1A 4WD
t: 020 7462 8000
f: 020 7462 6342

Building Design Partnership is one of Europe's leading multi-disciplinary architectural and engineering practices.

It has won many awards for the design and refurbishment of many buildings in different market sectors such as retail, education, industry, transport and leisure. With 6 UK offices and associations in France, Germany and Spain.

Responsible for Wimbledon's new No 1 Court and the flagship Marks & Spencer store in Manchester, the largest in the world.

Armed Forces

Army

www.armyofficer.co.uk

Alenia Marconi Systems . . . . www.aleniamarconisystems.com
Army . . . . www.armyofficer.co.uk
Devonport Royal Dockyard Ltd (DML). . . . . www.devonport.co.uk
GCHQ . . . . www.gchq.gov.uk

Royal Air Force

www.rafcareers.com

Royal Air Force . . . . www.rafcareers.com
Royal Naval Reserves . . . . www.royal-navy.mod.uk
Royal Navy . . . . www.rnjobs.co.uk
Territorial Army . . . . www.army.mod.uk/ta/

Royal Navy

www.rnjobs.co.uk
0845 607 5555

Dept 126, Freepost Royal Navy & Royal Marines,

Banks > Agencies

ABPM . . . . www.abpm.co.uk
Amery Cooper . . . . www.amerycooper.com

Parallel International

www.parallel-int.co.uk

1 Groveland Court, Bow Lane, London, EC4M 9EH
t: 020 7236 4288 **f:** 020 7236 4277

Aston Carter Ltd	www.astoncarter.com
Banking Additions	www.bankingadditions.com
City Jobs	www.cityjobs.com
Harrison Willis Ltd	www.hwgroup.co.uk
Hays Banking Personnel	www.haysworks.com
Hewitson Walker	www.hewitson-walker.co.uk
Lindsey Morgan Associates Ltd	www.lmassoc.com
Michael Page Group	www.michaelpage.net

The Graduate Recruitment Company

www.graduate-recruitment.co.uk

Alhambra House, 27-31 Charing Cross Road,
London, WC2H 0AU
t: 020 7565 3429

With more Banking vacancies than any other graduate recruitment agency in the UK we are The Graduate Recruitment Agency to deal with. More Jobs, more Employers, more choices.

Norman Broadbent. . . . . www.nb-selection.co.uk
Parallel International . . . . www.parallel-int.co.uk
The Graduate Recruitment Company . . . .
. . . . www.graduate-recruitment.co.uk
The Parker Bridge Group . . . . www.parkerbridge.com

Banks > Employers > Finance & Credit

Aegon Asset Management plc . . . . www.abetterway.com

Aegon Asset Management plc

www.abetterway.com

WWW.CHOICESONLINE.COM

Baillie Gifford

www.bailliegifford.com

1 Rutland Court, Edinburgh,
t: 0131 222 4000 **f:** 0131 222 4481

Business description: We are one of the UK's leading independent investment management firms. We are active fund managers and provide investment advice to some of the world's leading financial institutions.

N of vacancies: Approximately 8

Disciplines: If you have shown a consistently high level of academic achievement, then we would like to hear from you.

Application procedure: Please e-mail or post (at the above address) a current CV, or a standard application form, with a covering letter to Jane Paul at: graduates@bailliegifford.com

HSBC

www.hsbc.com/recruitment

The HSBC Group recruits graduates in the following areas:

Commercial banking
A minimum 2:2 in any discipline. The training programme includes the opportunity to study for the Associateship of the Chartered Institute of Banking qualification.

Information technology
A minimum 2:2 is required in any discipline. Project work is combined with classroom and on-the-job training to help you become an IT professional.

International management
Applicants need a 2:1 in any discipline. Applicants may be posted in any of the countries where the HSBC Group operates and are recruited as globally mobile generalist commercial bankers.

Investment banking and markets:
Applicants need 24 UCAS points and a 2:1 degree, preferably in a numerical or business-related subject. The graduate programme allows entry 'direct' into a chosen business area, or 'broad' rotations through 3 diverse business areas during the training period.

Further details on all these opportunities can be found on the website above.

WWW.CHOICESONLINE.COM

Baillie Gifford	www.bailliegifford.com
Barclays	www.barclays.co.uk
Bridge	www.bridge.com
CIBC World Markets	www.apply-cibcwm.co.uk
Ford Credit	www.fordcrediteurope.com
HSBC	www.hsbc.com/recruitment
MBNA International Bank Limited	www.mbna.com/europe

The Government Economic Service

020 7270 4581

HM Treasury, Parliament Street, London, SW1P 3AG
t: 020 7270 4581 **f:** 0171 270 4862

The GES is the largest UK employer of professional economists, with over 600 economists in 30 Government departments and agencies. GES memebers advise Ministers and Senior Administrators on a wide range of important economic issues across departments.

The Inland Revenue

www.inlandrevenue.gov.uk

Inland Revenue Graduate Recruitment Human Resources Division, Mowbray House PO Box 55 Castle Meadow Road, Nottingham, NG2 1BE
t: 0115 974 0606

N M Rothschild & Sons . . . . www.nmrothschild.com

Commerzbank

www.commerzbank.com/grads

NatWest plc . . . . www.rbs.co.uk/graduates
Royal & Sun Alliance plc . . . . www.ukgraduates.royalsun.com
Schroder Group plc . . . . www.schroders.com
The Government Economic Service . . . . www.ges.gov.uk
The Inland Revenue . . . . www.inlandrevenue.gov.uk
The Royal Bank of Scotland Group . . . . www.rbs.co.uk/graduates

Banks > Employers > Fund Managers

Fidelity Investments

Lehman Brothers

The Royal Bank of Scotland Group

www.rbs.co.uk/graduates

graduate.recruit@rbs.co.uk

Regent's House, PO Box 348,
42 Islington High Street, London, N1 8XL

t: 020 7615 32166

Training: Comprehensive and flexible training provided with sponsorship for professional qualifications

No. of vacancies: 300+

Disciplines: Applicants will need to have an Honours degree with a minimum class of 2:1 or 2:2 for some areas, any discipline

Application: Online via our graduate website

The Royal Bank of Scotland is one of Europe's largest, most dynamic and diverse financial services providers, incorporating such well know brands as NatWest, Direct Line, Green Flag and Coutts & Co.

The Graduate Development Programme, offers career opportunities in a variety of business areas such as: Corporate Banking, Financial Markets, Retail Banking, Technology, Finance, Internal Audit, HR and Retail Direct our card services and e-commerce division.

WWW.CHOICESONLINE.COM

Gartmore

www.gartmoregraduates.com

WWW.CHOICESONLINE.COM

Citigroup Corporate & Investment Bank/Schroder Salomon Smith Barney

www.citigroup.com/newgrads/recruits

33 Canada Square, Canary Wharf, London, E14 5LB
t: 020 7986 5309

Minimum required: Graduate level entry positions require a minimum 2:1 or equivalent. Any degree subject considered.

Application procedure: On-line application system via website.

Closing date: For full time applications, 30th November. For Summer Internship applications 28th February 2002. See website for exact dates.

Citigroup are a CORPORATE INVESTMENT BANK and the 3rd largest public finance company in the world.

Banks > Employers > Investment

Bank of England

www.jobsatthebank.co.uk

The Bank of England is the central bank of the UK.

A 2:1 degree in any discipline and an interest in economics and finance is essential .

Graduates join the Bank's Analyst Career Training (ACT) programme lasting 3 - 4 years.

For further information and to apply, please look at the Bank's website.

Bank of Scotland

www.bankofscotland.co.uk

graduate_recruitment@bank of scotland.co.uk

Bank of Scotland is known for excellent innovation and service within the financial industry and amongst customers, as well as offering challenging and rewarding careers to graduates.

N of vacancies: 30-40 to join our generalist training programme.

Disciplines involved Any degree discipline- more important are personality and transferable skills.

Salary: For 2000 basic ú17,000

Application procedure: Contact the Graduate Recruitment Team by telephone on 0131 243 0031

Barclays

www.barclays.com

www.graduatecareers.barclays.com

Barclays is a leading financial services organisation. Products and services include telephone banking and ISAs for personal customers, small and medium business banking and asset finance and investment solutions for multinational corporate customers.

Discipline: Applicants should ideally have a 2nd class honours degree in any subject and 22 UCAS points.

Opportunities: Graduate programmes exist in the following business areas and functions: Corporate Banking, Personal Financial Services and Barclays Private Clients, Africa, Barclaycard, Finance, Technology Solutions, Human Resources, Marketing and Risk.

HSBC

http://recruitment.hsbc.com

The HSBC Group recruits graduates in the following areas:

Commercial banking

A minimum of 14 UCAS points and a 2:2 in any discipline. The training programme includes the opportunity to study for the Associateship of the Chartered Institute of Banking qualification.

Information technology

A minimum 2:2 is required in any discipline. Project work is combined with classroom and on-the-job training to help you become an IT professional.

International management

Applicants need a 2:1 in any discipline. Applicants may be posted in any of the countries where the HSBC Group operates and are recruited as globally mobile generalist commercial bankers.

Investment banking and markets:

Applicants need 24 UCAS points and a 2:1 degree, preferably in a numerical or business-related subject. The graduate programme allows entry 'direct' into a chosen business area, or 'broad' rotations through 3 diverse business areas during the training period.

Further details on all these opportunities can be found on the website above.

WWW.CHOICESONLINE.COM

Bank of England. . . . . www.jobsatthebank.co.uk/
Bank of Scotland. . . . . www.bankofscotland.co.uk
Barclays . . . . www.barclays.com
Citigroup Corporate & Investment Bank/Schroder Salomon Smith Barney . . . .
. . . . www.citigroup.com
Commerzbank. . . . . www.commerzbank.com

The Royal Bank of Scotland Group

✖✖ The Royal Bank of
✖✖ Scotland Group

www.rbs.co.uk/graduates
graduate.recruit@rbs.co.uk

Regent's House, PO Box 348, 42 Islington High Street,
London, N1 8XL
t: 020 7615 32166

Training: Comprehensive and flexible training provided with
sponsorship for professional qualifications

No. of vacancies: 300+

Disciplines: Applicants will need to have an Honours degree
with a minimum class of 2:1 or 2:2 for some areas, any
discipline

Application: Online via our graduate website

The Royal Bank of Scotland is one of Europe's largest, most
dynamic and diverse financial services providers, incorporating
such well know brands as NatWest, Direct Line, Green Flag and
Coutts & Co.

The Graduate Development Programme, offers career
opportunities in a variety of business areas such as: Corporate
Banking, Financial Markets, Retail Banking, Technology,
Finance, Internal Audit, HR and Retail Direct our card services
and e-commerce division.

WWW.CHOICESONLINE.COM

Goldman Sachs & Co . . . . www.gs.com
HSBC . . . . www.hsbc.com/recruitment
ING Barings . . . . www.ingbarings.com/careers
J P Morgan . . . . www.jpmorgan.co.uk
Lehman Brothers . . . . www.lehman.com
Merrill Lynch & Co . . . . www.ml.com/careers

Tokyo-Mitsubishi International plc

 Tokyo-Mitsubishi International plc

020 7628 5555

6 Broadgate, London, EC2M 2AA
t: 020 7628 5555

Tokyo Mitsubishi International plc is the London investment banking arm of Japan's premier bank, The Bank of Tokyo-Mitsubishi, Ltd.

Graduates
We recruit graduates into the front office in Debt & Equity Markets, Structured Finance and Derivatives. Graduates tend to be placed into either sales or trading.

Training
Training programmes are tailored to individual requirements and generally last 4 - 7 months depending on progression and development. Mentors are assigned from each of the main business areas covered and this ensures that graduates gain the maximum benefit from the programme whilst getting regular feedback.

Requirements
We are looking for graduates who have strong mathematical and analytical skills with a 1st or 2:1 in related subjects. Language skills can be advantageous for certain departments although not a pre-requisite.

Further opportunities
Summer internships, lasting between 6 and 12 weeks are available in several business areas.

For further details on all opportunities and the application process, please refer to our website at www.t-mi.com.

WWW.CHOICESONLINE.COM

Merrill Lynch & Co

www.ml.com/careers

www.ml.com

Merrill Lynch is a leading global financial management and advisory company with a presence in 44 countries across six continents. We serve the needs of both individual and institutional clients with a diverse range of financial services.

Graduates:

Merrill Lynch recruits for over 150 full time and summer internship positions into the following areas: Debt Markets, Equity Markets, Investment Banking, Investment Managers, Research, Securities Services, Financial Operations, Human Resources and Technology.

The Deadline for full time applications is November 30th 2001 and for summer internship applications is February 15th 2002. All applications must be received online, but please be aware that applications will be dealt with on a first come first served basis, so early application may be advantageous.

Full details of all the graduate programmes, and our online application form can be found on our website - www.ml.com/careers

WWW.CHOICESONLINE.COM

Banks > Employers > Retail

Abbey National plc

www.abbeynational.plc.uk/recruitment

Abbey House, 201 Grafton Gate East, Milton Keynes,
MK9 1AN
t: 0870 6000 860

Alliance & Leicester plc . . . . www.alliance-leicester.co.uk

Barclays

BARCLAYS
www.graduatecareers.barclays.com

www.barclays.com
www.graduatecareers.barclays.com

Graduate Recruitment, First Floor,
155 Bishopsgate, London, EC2M 3XA
t: 020 7699 5000

Barclays is a leading financial services organisation. Products
and services include telephone banking and ISAs for personal
customers, small and medium business banking and asset
finance and investment solutions for multinational corporate
customers.

Discipline
Applicants should ideally have a 2nd class honours degree in any
subject and 22 UCAS points.

Opportunities
Graduate programmes exist in the following business areas and
functions: Corporate Banking, Personal Financial Services and
Barclays Private Clients, Africa, Barclaycard, Finance,
Technology Solutions, Human Resources, Marketing and Risk.

HSBC

HSBC ◆

http://recruitment.hsbc.com

The HSBC Group recruits graduates in the following areas:

Commercial banking
A minimum of 14 UCAS points and a 2:2 in any discipline. The training programme includes the opportunity to study for the Associateship of the Chartered Institute of Banking qualification.

Information technology
A minimum 2:2 is required in any discipline. Project work is combined with classroom and on-the-job training to help you become an IT professional.

International management
Applicants need a 2:1 in any discipline. Applicants may be posted in any of the countries where the HSBC Group operates and are recruited as globally mobile generalist commercial bankers.

Investment banking and markets:
Applicants need 24 UCAS points and a 2:1 degree, preferably in a numerical or business-related subject. The graduate programme allows entry 'direct' into a chosen business area, or 'broad' rotations through 3 diverse business areas during the training period.

Further details on all these opportunities can be found on the website above.

Nationwide Building Society

www.nationwide.co.uk

Nationwide House, Pipers Way, Swindon, SN38 1NW

The Royal Bank of Scotland Group

www.rbs.co.uk/graduates
graduate.recruit@rbs.co.uk

Regent's House, PO Box 348, 42 Islington High Street,
London, N1 8XL
t: 020 7615 32166

Training: Comprehensive and flexible training provided with sponsorship for professional qualifications

No. of vacancies: 300+

Disciplines: Applicants will need to have an Honours degree with a minimum class of 2:1 or 2:2 for some areas, any discipline

Application: Online via our graduate website

The Royal Bank of Scotland is one of Europe's largest, most dynamic and diverse financial services providers, incorporating such well know brands as NatWest, Direct Line, Green Flag and Coutts & Co.

The Graduate Development Programme, offers career opportunities in a variety of business areas such as: Corporate Banking, Financial Markets, Retail Banking, Technology, Finance, Internal Audit, HR and Retail Direct our card services and e-commerce division.

WWW.CHOICESONLINE.COM

Barclays . . . . www.barclays.com
Clydesdale Bank plc . . . . www.cbonline.co.uk
Cooperative bank . . . . www.cooperativebank.co.uk
Girobank . . . . www.girobank.co.uk
Halifax plc . . . . www.halifax.co.uk
HSBC . . . . www.hsbc.com/recruitment

Yorkshire Building Society

www.ybs.co.uk

Yorkshire House, Yorkshire Drive, Bradford,
West Yorkshire, BD5 8LJ
t: 01274 472 435 **f:** 01274 395 474

Business description: Yorkshire Building Society is a leading mutual Building Society with it's head office in Bradford and a national network of branches and agencies.

N of vacancies: Varies. Opportunities across the UK in branches or at HO office in Bradford.

Opportunities available: We look for graduates with 1-2 years commercial experience after graduation to join us on a one year development programme.

Application procedure: Send us a full and up-to-date CV along with a covering letter to the above address.

More company information is available on our web-site at: www.ybs.co.uk

WWW.CHOICESONLINE.COM

Lloyds TSB . . . . www.lloydstsb.co.uk
Nationwide Building Society . . . . www.nationwide.co.uk
NatWest plc . . . . www.rbs.co.uk/graduates
Northern Rock plc . . . . www.northernrock.co.uk
The Royal Bank of Scotland Group . . . . www.rbs.co.uk/graduates
West Bromwich Building society . . . . www.westbrom.co.uk
Woolwich plc . . . . www.thewoolich.co.uk
Yorkshire Building Society . . . . www.ybs.co.uk

Banks > Institutes & Media

Chartered Institute of Bankers. . . . . www.cib.org.uk
Chartered Institute of Bankers in Scotland. . . . www.ciobs.org.uk
Institute of Credit Management. . . . . www.icm.org.uk

Chartered Institute of Bankers in Scotland

www.ciobs.org.uk

19 Rutland Square, Edinburgh, EH1 2DE
t: 0131 473 7777

Institute of Credit Management

www.icm.org.uk

The Water Mill, Station Road, South Luffenham,
Oakham, LE15 8NB
t: 01780 722 906 **f:** 01780 721 271

Construction > Building Companies

AYH plc. . . . . www.ayh.com
Bechtel . . . . www.bechtel.co.uk
Bechtel Ltd. . . . . www.bechtel.co.uk
Building Design Partnership . . . . www.bdp.co.uk
Chartered Institute of Building. . . . . www.ciob.org.uk
Clugston Construction . . . . www.clugston.co.uk

AYH plc

www.ayh.com

40 Clifton Street, London, EC2A 4AY
t: 020 7377 6666

London (Head Office), Birmingham, Manchester, Leeds, Edinburgh

AYH plc are property and construction consultants providing project management, cost consultancy and quantity surveying, facilities consultancy, building surveying, engineering services consultancy and CDM compliance services to clients in the UK and overseas.

Chartered Institute of Building

www.ciob.org.uk

Englemere, Kings Ride, Ascot, Berkshire, SL5 7TB
t: 01344 630 700 **f:** 01344 630 777

The Chartered Institute of Building is the professional body for today's managers in construction.

The Institute has almost 40,000 members, skilled managers and professionals drawn from the top ranks of the construction industry, with a common commitment to achieve and maintain the highest possible standards.

Bechtel

www.bechtel.co.uk

245 Hammersmith Road, London, W6 8DP

Clugston Construction

www.clugston.co.uk

St. Vincent House, NormanbyRoad, Scunthorpe, DN15 8QT
t: 01724 843 491 **f:** 01724 867 680

A private company established over 60 years ago employing over 600 employees engaged in building, civil engineering, contracting and plant and tool hire.

EC Harris	www.echarris.com
Edmund Nuttall Ltd	www.edmund-nuttall.co.uk
Mott MacDonald	www.mottmac.co.uk
MW Kellogg Limited	www.mwkl.co.uk
Norwest Holst Group PLC	www.norwest-holst.co.uk

EC Harris

www.echarris.com
opportunities@echarris.com
information@echarris.com

Lynton House, 7-12 Tavistock Square, London, WC1H 9LX
t: 020 7387 8431 **f:** 020 7391 3850

EC Harris is at the forefront of the construction, real estate and engineering industries, with offices worldwide.

MW Kellogg Limited

M W Kellogg Limited

www.mwkl.co.uk
opportunities@mwkl.co.uk

Kellogg Tower, Greenford Road,
Greenford, Middlesex, UB6 0JA
t: 020 8872 7000

Business description:
MW Kellogg Ltd is a global engineering and construction company working within the Petrochemical industry.

No of vacancies:
We have approximately 20-25 vacancies.

Opportunities available:
At MW Kellogg you will follow a two year rotational training programme which guarantees chartership. Your training will also be supplemented with internal and external courses in both technical and business disciplines.

Application procedure:
E-mail us your CV opportunities@mwkl.co.uk More information on the company and our recruitment selection process is available on our web-site at www.mwkl.co.uk

Ove Arup

www.arup.com

Chancery House, 53-64 Chancery Lane, London, WC2A 1QS

Norwest Holst Group PLC

www.norwest-holst.co.uk
group.hr@norwest.co.uk

Astral House, Imperial Way, Watford, WD24 4WW

Business description: Norwest Holst is one of the UK's leading contractors, providing an exceptional and diverse range of skills across all the principal sectors of the construction industry.

Opportunities available: We provide a competitive salary and benefits, relevant training and continuous professional development opportunities.

Application procedure: Application forms are available on-line, alternatively, you can send us a full and up-to-date CV along with a covering letter to the above address.

More information on the company and our recruitment process is available on our web-site at www.norwest-holst.co.uk

The Miller Group

www.miller.co.uk

Miller House, 18 South Groathill Avenue, Edinburgh,
EH4 2LW

The Miller Group is the UK's largest privately owned property development, house building and construction services company.

A structured graduate training programme is in place leading to Chartered status. Opportunities for further study through the Miller Management Development Programme.

Apply on-line or send CV with covering letter to the Staff Development Manager or telephone 0131 315 6272.

Construction > Consultant Engineers

Aspen Consulting Group

www.aspenconsult.co.uk
ggreenland@aspenconsult.co.uk

Dippen Hall Eastbourne Road,
Blindley Heath, Lingfield, Surrey, RH7 6JX
t: 01342 893 800

Application procedure: Send your CV to: Glynis Greenland at the above address or e-mail it to ggreenland@aspenconsult .co.uk

Vacancy locations: Vacancies in the Home Counties, London and the South East, South West, Midlands, North East, North West and Scotland.

Aspen Consulting Group Ltd is a multi-disciplinary company of Consulting Engineers and Quantity Surveyors which has achieved a remarkably successful growth rate since it was established in the late 1980's. The company currently has a staff level of approximately 410, providing clients with an efficient, professional service tailored to meet client requirements and constraints. Our client list includes such names as: WS Atkins, Balfour Beatty and Railtrack.

AYH plc

www.ayh.com

40 Clifton Street, London, EC2A 4AY
t: 020 7377 6666

London (Head Office), Birmingham, Manchester, Leeds, Edinburgh

AYH plc are property and construction consultants providing project management, cost consultancy and quantity surveying, facilities consultancy, building surveying, engineering services consultancy and CDM compliance services to clients in the UK and overseas.

EC Harris

EC HARRIS

Capital Project and Facilities Consultants

www.echarris.com

Lynton House, 7-12 Tavistock Square, London, WC1H 9LX
t: 020 7387 8431 **f:** 020 7391 3850

Offering graduates: Interesting and Challenging work. Competitive salaries. Continual skills development and training.

Find out more: For further information on graduate opportunities email: information@echarris.com

EC Harris are at the forefront of the construction, real estate and engineering entries.

Buro Happold

Buro Happold
Engineers

www.burohappold.com
recruitment@burohappold.com

Camden Mill, Lower Bristol Road, Bath, BA2 3DQ
t: 01225 320 600 **f:** 01225 320 701

N of vacancies: 40 graduate vacancies.

Disciplines involved: Structural engineering, civil and structural engineering, civil engineering, civil engineering with architecture, building services engineering, building engineering, quantity surveying.

Buro Happold has job openings in the following areas: Structural, Civil, Mechanical and Electrical, Building Services, Facades, Geotechnical/Ground Engineering, Fire Engineering, Access, Project Management & Cost Engineering.

Locations: Bath, London, Leeds, Glasgow, Manchester, Cardiff, Berlin, Dublin, Riyadh, Singapore, New York, Warsaw.

Application procedure: For more information please contact us for a graduate brochure and application form. Visit our website at www.burohappold.com for further details of the recruitment process and closing date.

Buro Happold is a dynamic practice of consulting engineers with a reputation for imaginative engineering. We are known for designs that present buildability, sustainability, efficient use of materials and energy resulting in added value to the client. Our approach to complex construction problems puts us at the leading edge of the industry. Good design is the result of genuine harmony between the artistic, the scientific and the practical. These principles govern Buro Happold's work and the distinctly unique culture of the practice, currently 750 strong worldwide.

Max Fordham LLP

www.maxfordham.com

42/43 Gloucester Crescent, London, NW1 7PE
t: 020 7267 5161

We are a leading firm of environmental and building services
consulting engineers with projects in the UK and abroad.

WS Atkins

www.whywsatkins.com
info@wsatkins.com

Woodcote Grove, Ashley Road, Epsom, Surrey, KT18 5BW

WS Atkins is one of the worldÆs leading providers of
professional, technology-based consultancy and support
services. Our success is built on the talents and commitment of
our people.

In return, we offer exciting opportunities for career development in
the areas of technical specialism, project management, business
development and operational management, within a dynamic and
strongly entrepreneurial company.

web site: www.whywsatkins.com

Mouchel

www.mouchel.com

PA Consulting Group

www.paconsulting.com

123 Buckingham Palace Road, London, SW1W 9SR
t: 020 7730 9000

London (Head Office), and worldwide.

PA Consulting Group is a leading management, systems, and technology consulting firm.

We are particularly interested in recruiting into the following areas:

Technology & Innovation: This is where we develop award-winning products, automation and manufacturing processes that will transform the contribution that technology makes to businesses.

Strategy & Industries: Strategy & Marketing, Telecoms & Interactive Media, Financial Services and Government & Public Services.

IT: Systems Development, IT Management, IT Infrastructure and IT strategy (management sciences).

WWW.CHOICESONLINE.COM

Anglian Water Engineering . . . . www.anglianwater.co.uk
Aspen Consulting Group. . . . . www.aspenconsult.co.uk
AYH plc. . . . . www.ayh.com
Babtie Group . . . . www.babtie.com
Buro Happold . . . . www.burohappold.com
Campbell Reith Hill . . . . www.campbellreith.com
Clancy Consulting . . . . www.clancy.co.uk
EC Harris . . . . www.echarris.com
GIBB Ltd. . . . . www.gibbltd.com
Halcrow. . . . . www.halcrow.com
Helios Technology . . . . www.helios-tech.co.uk
Hulley and Kirkwood . . . . www.hulley.co.uk
Intec (u.k.) Ltd. . . . . www.intecm.co.uk
Max Fordham LLP . . . . www.maxfordham.com

Mott MacDonald

www.mottmac.co.uk

graduate.recruitment@mottmac.com

Demeter House, Station Road, Cambridge, CB1 2RS
t: 01223 463 657/58

WWW.CHOICESONLINE.COM

Posford Duvivier

www.posford.co.uk

WWW.CHOICESONLINE.COM

Construction > Quantity Surveyors

Davis Langdon & Everest

www.davislangdon.com

Princes House, 39 Kingsway, London, WC2B 6TP
t: 020 7497 9000

19 offices throughout the UK including; London, Manchester, Cambridge, Bristol and Glasgow.

Davis Langdon & Everest is one of the world's leading firms of Chartered Quantity Surveyors. They provide innovative and proactive professional services via advanced technical support systems.

Davis Langdon & Everest . . . . www.davislangdon.com

EC Harris

EC HARRIS

Capital Project and Facilities Consultants

www.echarris.com
opportunities@echarris.com
information@echarris.com

Lynton House, 7-12 Tavistock Square, London, WC1H 9LX
t: 020 7387 8431 **f:** 020 7391 3850

Offices: Throughout the UK and worldwide.

EC Harris is a leading Capital Project and Facilities Consultant at the forefront of the construction, real estate and engineering industry.

Gardiner & Theobald

www.gardiner.com
s.hawkins@gardiner.com

32 Bedford Square, London, WC1B 3JT
t: 020 7209 3000

Gardiner & Theobald are leading quantity surveyors with offices London (Head Office), Belfast, Birmingham, Bristol, Cardiff, Dublin, Edinburgh, Glasgow, Leeds, Manchester, Newcastle, Scunthorpe and Swindon.

Graduates can apply on-line or download the application form and send to Susie Hawkins at the above address.

WWW.CHOICESONLINE.COM

Education

Geos Language

www.geocareer.com

The Personnel Department, Compton Park, Compton Place Road, Eastbourne, BN21 1EH

Established in 1973, GEOS is Japan's most respected provider of English Language and cultural education. Our expanding network includes almost 500 schools in Japan and 40 in other countries.

WWW.CHOICESONLINE.COM

VSO

www.vso.org.uk

317 Putney Bridge Road, London, SW15 2PN

Types of work offered: Teaching, Teacher Training and Education Management placements covering Primary, Secondary, Further and Higher Education. Teaching placements normally focus on Maths, Science, English and those with special needs.

N of vacancies: Over 500 placements a year open to those with either qualified teacher status or with appropriate TEFL, City and Guilds or other prof. Qualifications

Opportunities available: The chance to share skills with local communities in over 50 developing countries worldwide, make lasting friendships and return enriched personally and professionally by the experience.

Support from VSO: Quality training and support, return airfares, medical cover, salary, benefits payment, grants.

Further information: Website: for placement information and events. Email enquiry@vso.org.uk. Ring someone who's been there and done it: 0845 603 0027 or our Enquiry unit on 020 8780 7500, mini-com 020 8780 7440.

Inlingua Teacher Training

www.inligua-cheltenham.co.uk
recruitment@inligua-cheltenham.co.uk

Department for Education and Employment

department for
education and skills
creating opportunity, releasing potential, achieving excellence

www.dfee.gov.uk

Coxton House, 6-12 Tothill Street, London, SW19 9NF
t: 020 7273 3000

The Department of Education and Employment is a UK Government department. Our aim is to give everyone the opportunity to fulfill their potential through education, training and work.

We have vacancies for administrators, managers, research assistants, senior managers and public appointments.

Details of all our vacancies can be found on the website above.

Education > Local Authorities

Birmingham

www.birmingham.gov.uk

Council House Extension, Margaret Street,
Birmingham, B3 3BU
t: 0121 303 2872 f: 0121 303 1318

Bexley	www.bexley.gov.uk
Birmingham	www.birmingham.gov.uk
Blackburn with Darwen	www.blackburn.gov.uk
Blackpool	www.blackpool.gov.uk
Bolton	www.bolton.gov.uk
Bournemouth	www.bournemouth.gov.uk
Bracknell Forest	www.bracknell-forest.gov.uk
Bradford	www.bradford.gov.uk
Brent	www.brent.gov.uk
Brighton & Hove	www.brighton-hove.gov.uk
Bristol	www.bristol-city.gov.uk
Bromley	www.bromley.gov.uk
Buckinghamshire	www.buckscc.gov.uk
Bury	www.bury.gov.uk
Calderdale	www.calderdale.gov.uk
Cambridgeshire	www.camcnty.gov.uk
Camden	www.camden.gov.uk
Cheshire	www.cheshire.gov.uk
City of London	www.cityoflondon.gov.uk
Cleveland	www.cornwall.gov.uk
Coventry	www.coventry.gov.uk
Croydon	www.croydon.gov.uk
Cumbria	www.cumbria.gov.uk
Darlington	www.darlington.gov.uk
Derby	www.derby.gov.uk
Derbyshire	www.derbyshire.gov.uk
Devon	www.devon.gov.uk
Doncaster	www.doncaster.gov.uk
Dorset	www.dorset-cc.gov.uk
Dudley	www.dudley.gov.uk
Durham	www.durham.gov.uk
Ealing	www.ealing.gov.uk
East Riding of Yorkshire	www.east-riding-of-yorkshire.gov.uk
East Sussex	www.eastsussexcc.gov.uk
Enfield	www.enfield.gov.uk

Hammersmith and Fulham

www.lbhf.gov.uk

Cambridge Grove, Hammersmith, London, W6 0LE
t: 020 8748 3020 x 3621 **f:** 020 8576 5686

Essex . . . . www.essexcc.gov.uk
Gateshead . . . . www.gateshead.gov.uk
Gloucestershire. . . . . www.gloscc.gov.uk
Greenwich. . . . . www.greenwich.gov.uk
Hackney. . . . . www.hackney.gov.uk
Halton . . . . www.halton.gov.uk
Hammersmith and Fulham . . . . www.lbhf.gov.uk
Hampshire . . . . www.hants.gov.uk
Haringey . . . . www.haringey.gov.uk
Harrow. www.harrowlb.demon.co.uk
Hartlepool . . . . www.hartlepool.gov.uk
Havering . . . . www.havering.gov.uk
Herefordshire . . . . www.herefordshire.gov.uk
Hertfordshire . . . . www.hertscc.gov.uk
Hillingdon . . . . www.hillingdon.gov.uk
Hounslow . . . . www.hounslow.gov.uk
Isle of wight . . . . www.iwight.gov.uk
Isles of scilly. 0
Islington . . . . www.islington.gov.uk
Kensington and Chelsea . . . . www.rbkc.gov.uk
Kent . . . . www.kent.gov.uk
Kingston upon Hull. www.hullcc.gov.uk
Kingston upon Thames . . . . www.kingston.gov.uk
Kirklees. . . . . www.kirkleesmc.gov.uk
Knowsley . . . . www.knowsley.gov.uk
Lancashire . . . . www.lancashire.gov.uk
Leeds . . . . www.leeds.gov.uk

Leicestershire

www.leics.gov.uk

County Hall, Glenfield, Leicester, LE3 8RF
t: 0116 232 3232 **f:** 0116 265 6634

Leicester City . . . . www.leicester.gov.uk/city/
Leicestershire . . . . www.leics.gov.uk
Lewisham . . . . www.lewisham.gov.uk
Lincolnshire . . . . www.lincolnshire.gov.uk
Liverpool . . . . www.liverpool.gov.uk
Luton . . . . www.luton.gov.uk
Manchester . . . . www.manchester.gov.uk
Medway . . . . www.medway.gov.uk
Merton . . . . www.merton.gov.uk
Middlesbrough . . . . www.middlesbrough.gov.uk
Milton keynes . . . . www.mkweb.co.uk
Newcastle upon Tyne . . . . www.newcastle.gov.uk
Newham . . . . www.newham.gov.uk
Norfolk . . . . www.norfolk.gov.uk
North east Lincolnshire . . . . www.nelincs.gov.uk
North Lincolnshire . . . . www.northlincs.gov.uk
North Somerset . . . . www.n-somerset.gov.uk
North Tyneside . . . . www.northtyneside.gov.uk
North Yorkshire . . . . www.northyorks.gov.uk
Northamptonshire . . . . www.northants-ecl.gov.uk
Northumberland . . . . www.northumberland.gov.uk
Nottingham . . . . www.nottinghamcity.gov.uk
Nottinghamshire . . . . www.nottscc.gov.uk
Oldham . . . . www.oldham.gov.uk

Tameside

www. ⫘ **Tameside** .gov.uk

www.tameside.gov.uk

Council Offices, Wellington Road, Ashton-under-Lyne,
OL6 6DL
t: 0161 342 8355 **f:** 0161 342 3260

Southampton	www.southampton.gov.uk
Southend-on-Sea	www.southend.gov.uk
Southwark	www.southwark.gov.uk
St helens	www.sthelens.gov.uk
Staffordshire	www.stafford.gov.uk
Stockport	www.stockportmbc.gov.uk
Stockton-on-Tees	www.train.stockton.gov.uk
Stoke-on-Trent	www.stoke.gov.uk
Suffolk	www.suffolkcc.gov.uk
Sunderland	www.sunderland.gov.uk
Surrey	www.surreycc.gov.uk
Sutton	www.sutton.gov.uk
Swindon	www.swindon.gov.uk
Tameside	www.tameside.gov.uk
Telford and Wrekin	www.telford.gov.uk
Thurrock	www.thurrock.gov.uk/education
Torbay	www.torbay.gov.uk
Tower Hamlets	www.towerhamlets.gov.uk
Trafford	www.trafford.gov.uk
Wakefield	www.wakefield.gov.uk
Walsall	www.walsall.gov.uk
Waltham Forest	www.lbwf.gov.uk
Wandsworth	www.wandsworth.gov.uk
Warrington	www.warrington.gov.uk
Warwickshire	www.warwickshire.gov.uk
West Berkshire	www.westberks.gov.uk
West Sussex	www.westsussex.gov.uk
Westminster	www.westminster.gov.uk
Wigan	www.wiganmbc.gov.uk
Wiltshire	www.wiltshire.gov.uk
Windsor and Maidenhead	www.rbwm.gov.uk
Wirral	www.wirral.gov.uk
Wokingham	www.wokingham.gov.uk
Wolverhampton City Council	www.wolverhampton.gov.uk
Worcestershire	www.worcestershire.gov.uk

Engineering

Air Products PLC

www.airproducts.com

Hersham Place, Molesey Road,
Walton-on-Thames, Surrey, KT12 4RZ
t: 01932 249 200 **f:** 01932 249 565

N of vacancies: Approx.25 vacancies

Disciplines involved: Chemical, mechanical and electrical engineering, sciences and technology, computer sciences, finance, business, marketing.

Recruited to: Engineering, Sales, Marketing, Finance, Information Technology, Manufacturing, Procurement, Chemicals, R & D.

Locations: Through UK and Europe - mobility important and languages useful

Application procedure: Please contact career services, visit our website or call us. For an application form please see our website.

Air products PLC is part of the major international group of Air Products and Chemicals founded in 1940 in the USA. Today, the Group has an annual turnover approaching ú5 billion and employs over 16,000 people in 30 countries, including over 5,000 in Europe.

Agilent Technologies

www.agilentgraduates.co.uk

Airbus UK

www.airbus-careers.com

Young People Services Adviser, New Filton House, Filton, Bristol, BS99 7AR

Airbus UK . . . . www.airbus-careers.com
Aircom International . . . . www.aircom.co.uk
Alenia Marconi Systems . . . . www.aleniamarconisystems.com
Amec . . . . www.amec.com
Atomic Weapons Establishment plc . . . . www.awe.co.uk
Avesta Polarit . . . . www.avestapolarit.com
BAE Systems . . . . www.baesystems.com
Balfour Beatty Ltd . . . . www.balfourbeatty.com

Aircom International

www.aircom.co.uk

Avesta Polarit

www.avestapolarit.com

Atomic Weapons Establishment plc

www.awe.co.uk

Alenia Marconi Systems

www.aleniamarconisystems.com
isd.recruitment@amsjv.com

Lyon Way, Frimley Road, Camberley, Surrey, GU16 5EX
t: 01276 63311

Have you ever wondered how a missile reaches it's target or how planes fly safely through the sky? Are you an Engineer interested in working at the cutting edge of the defence and electronics industry?

If the answer is yes, Alenia Marconi may have an opportunity for you. We are looking for Software, Hardware and System Engineers to join a world leader in the provision of integrated defence and electronic systems solutions.

With a customer base in over 100 countries, we are acknowledged experts in ground and naval radar, missile systems, air traffic management, command and control, simulation and synthetic environments, engineering, software design and manufacturing.

Bombardier Transportation

www.transportation.bombardier.com

Litchurch Lane, Derby, DE24 8AD
t: 01332 266 398

Bookham Technology

www.bookham.com

Caterpillar

www.cat.com

Shared Servicxes, Vicarage Farm Road Office, Eastfield,
Peterborough, PE1 5NA
t: 01733 584 640

Computing Devices Company Ltd

www.computingdevices.co.uk
gdrecruitment@compd.com

Castleham Road, St Leonards on sea, East Sussex,
TN38 9NJ
t: 01424 853481 **f:** 01424 798467

DSTL

www.dstl..gov.uk

Devonport Royal Dockyard Ltd (DML)

www.devonport.co.uk
dml.recruitment@devonport.co.uk

Devonport Royal Dockyard, Plymouth, PL1 4SG
t: 01752 605 665

Dyson Ltd

www.dyson.com

Tetbury Hill, Malmesbury, Wiltshire, SN16 ORP
t: 01666 828280

European Patent Office

www.epo.org
recruitment.munich@epo.org
recruitment.berlin@epo.org
recruitment.thehague@epo.org

FKI plc

www.fki.co.uk

PO Box 18, Loughborough, Leics, LE11 1HJ
t: 01509 617959 **f:** 01509 612812

Business description: FKI is now a world force in engineering employing over 17,000 people in 40 countries in 22 principal subsidiaries. It has world leading positions in its specialised business areas: Logistex, Energy Technology, Lifting Products & Services and Hardware.

N of vacancies: We have 15-20 vacancies for qualified graduates annually.

Opportunities available: All FKI companies offer a range of opportunities in engineering design, development, manufacturing, quality control, sales, marketing, and IT.

Application procedure: Application forms are available on-line at the web-site below.

More information can be found on-line at: www.fki.co.uk

GKN plc

GKN plc

THE GKN INTERNATIONAL LEADERSHIP DEVELOPMENT PROGRAMME

www.ildp.gknplc.com

sharon.goymer@gknplc.com

PO Box 55, Redditch, Worcestershire, B98 0TL
t: 01527 533 393 **f:** 01527 533 474

Business description: We are a global engineering company with operations in over 30 countries.

N of vacancies: We have 40 vacancies worldwide.

Opportunities available: We have an individual training programme for Engineers and Business/Management graduates with the opportunity to learn a new language and spend at least six months abroad, all within the first two years of joining.

Application procedure: Apply on-line or request a brochure through our web-site www.ildp.gknplc.com

More information about GKN plc and the ILDP can be found on our web-site www.ildp.gknplc.com

HM Government Communication Centre

www.hmgcc.gov.uk

Hanslope Park, Hanslope, Milton Keynes, MK19 6BH
t: 01908 510052

Imagination Technologies

www.imgtec.com

Home Park Estate, Kings Langley, Herts, WD4 8LZ
t: 01923 260511

Infraco BCV Ltd

www.ibcv.co.uk

Linn Products. . . . . www.linn.co.uk
MW Kellogg Limited . . . . www.mwkl.co.uk
National Air Traffic Service. . . . . www.nats.co.uk/recruitment

Jaguar Cars Ltd

www.careers.jaguar.com
jaggrad@jaguar.com

Kraft Foods UK Ltd

www.kraft.com

Human Resources Department, Banbury, Oxford, OX16 2QU

Laing Utilities

www.laing.com

Barford Road, St Neots, Cambs, PE19 6WB
t: 01480 402500

WWW.CHOICESONLINE.COM

Land Rover

www.landrovercareers.com

WWW.CHOICESONLINE.COM

Linn Products

www.linn.co.uk

Floors Road, Waterfoot, Glasgow, G76 6PE
t: 0141 307 7777

WWW.CHOICESONLINE.COM

National Grid Company plc . . . . www.nationalgrid.com/uk/careers
National Semiconductor . . . . www.national.com
Norwest Holst Group plc . . . . www.norwest-holst.co.uk
Novar . . . . www.novar.com
Oracle Corporation UK Ltd . . . . jobs.oracle.com/graduates
Oscar Faber . . . . www.oscarfaber.com
Philips Electronics UK Limited . . . . www.philips.co.uk

National Semiconductor

www.national.com

Earnhill Road, Larkfield Industrial Estate, Greenock,
PA16 0EQ
t: 01475 633733 **f:** 01475 639366

WWW.CHOICESONLINE.COM

MW Kellogg Limited

in MW Kellogg Limited

www.mwkl.co.uk
opportunities@mwkl.co.uk

Kellogg Tower, Greenford Road,
Greenford, Middlesex, UB6 0JA
t: 020 8872 7000

Business description:
MW Kellogg Ltd is a global engineering and construction company working within the Petrochemical industry.

No of vacancies:
We have approximately 20-25 vacancies.

Opportunities available:
At MW Kellogg you will follow a two year rotational training programme which guarantees chartership. Your training will also be supplemented with internal and external courses in both technical and business disciplines.

Application procedure:
E-mail us your CV opportunities@mwkl.co.uk More information on the company and our recruitment selection process is available on our web-site at www.mwkl.co.uk

National Air Traffic Service

www.nats.co.uk/recruitment

Recruitment Services, T1213, One Kemble Street, London,
WC2B 4AP
t: 020 7832 5555

National Grid Company plc

www.nationalgrid.com/uk/careers
graduate.jobs@uk.ngrid.com

Kirby Corner Road, Coventry, CV4 8JY
t: 024 7642 3374 **f:** 024 7642 3413

A FTSE 100 company National Grid is the world's leading transmission company.

Graduates in Electrical/Electronic/Power Systems Engineering, Business Studies, Physics, Economics, Mathematics and IT are welcome to apply. A world of opportunity awaits you!

Applications are welcome on-line or can be sent to the above address.

Novar

www.novar.com

Novar House, 24 Queens Road, Weybridge, KT13 9UX
t: 0800 013 1002

Oscar Faber

www.oscarfaber.com

Marlborough House, Upper Marlborough Road, St Albans, Herts, AL1 3UT
t: 020 8784 5784

Norwest Holst Group plc

www.norwest-holst.co.uk

Ditton Road, Widness, Cheshire, WA8 0WE
t: 0151 422 3940 **f:** 0151 424 9501

Business description: Norwest Holst is one of the UK's leading contractors, providing an exceptional and diverse range of skills across all the principal sectors of the construction industry.

Opportunities available: We provide a competitive salary and benefits, relevant training and continuous professional development opportunities.

Application procedure: Application forms are available on-line, alternatively, you can send us a full and up-to-date CV along with a covering letter to the above address.

More information on the company and our recruitment process is available on our web-site at www.norwest-holst.co.uk

Oracle Corporation UK Ltd

jobs.oracle.com/graduates

Recruitment Dept, Oracle Parkway, Thames Valley Park,
Reading, Berks, RG6 1RA
t: 0118 924 5572

Subjects of study: Applications Consultancy degree. Others: IT related degree. Ideally 2:1 or above.

Work offered: Technical or Applications Consulting, Product development (designer/developer 2000 and applications).

Locations: Reading and Hemel Hempstead

Application is through the website only.

Oracle are a leading supplier of software information, technology services and solutions.

Philips Electronics UK Limited

www.philips.co.uk

PO Box 391, Richmond, Surrey, TW9 2XZ

Snell & Wilcox . . . . www.snellwilcox.com
Symonds Group Ltd . . . . www.symonds-group.com

Ricardo

www.ricardo.com

Bridge Works, Shoreham-by-Sea, West Sussex, BN43 5FG
t: 01273 455 611

Power Engineering Consultants plc

www.pecplc.com

Jameson House, 11a London Road,
Alderley Edge, Cheshire, SK9 7JT
t: 01625 586 808 **f:** 01625 584 728

Vacancies for electrical engineering honour graduates who have done power systems in final year to train as power plant commissioning engineers.

A good knowledge of electrical principles, a 2.1 degree or exceptional 2.2 and a willingness to travel world-wide are all essential.

Vacancies also for trainee protection and earthing designers and planners. Similar qualifications required.

Roger Preston & Partners

www.rpreston.com

29 Broadway, Maidenhead, Berkshire, SL6 1LY
t: 01628 623 423

Smiths Group

www.smiths-group.com

765 Finchley Road, London, NW11 8DS
t: 020 8458 3232 **f:** 020 8209 0514

London (Head Office), c.40,000 employees, 40 countries

4 principal divisions: Medical, Industrial, Aerospace, Sealing Solutions

Disciplines involved: Engineering, management, HR, IT, marketing.

Shell

www.shell.com
www.shell.com/careers
Response@si.shell.com

Rowlandsway House, Rowlandsway,
Manchester, M22 5SB
t: 0845 600 1819 **f:** 0161 499 4859

N of vacancies: We have approximately 500 graduate vacancies worldwide.

Disciplines involved: Any discipline will be considered although for Technical vacancies a relevant degree subject is required.

Type of work offered: Engineering, Finance, Marketing and Sales, Supply Chain, Information Technology, eBusiness, Human Resources, Trading and Research.

Locations: Over 120 countries worldwide.

Application procedure: For an application form visit our website or telephone 0845 600 1819.

Shell is at the heart of the energy and petrochemical business, and one of the world's most successful organisations. Our business is unique. It not only has a huge impact on global development, but also offers international career prospects and outstanding challenges.

The Patent Office

www.patent.gov.uk
enquiries@patent.gov.uk

Snell & Wilcox

Engineering With Vision

www.snellwilcox.com
info@snellwilcox.com

Durford Mill, Petersfield, Hampshire, GU31 5AZ
t: 01730 818700

Snell & Wilcox is an award-winning engineering-led company with a reputation for high quality digital image processing products.

Petersfield, Liss, Havant, Saffron Walden

Disciplines involved: Electronics. Engineering, computer science, physics, mathematics or similar for engineering careers; any discipline for non engineering.

Training Given: Mixture of formal and informal training, in-company presentations, flexibility to move within company.

Siemens plc

www.siemens.co.uk
siemens.grad@plcman.siemens.co.uk

Siemens plc, established in 1843, is one of the world's largest electrical, electronic and communication firms.

For further information visit the website. Applications are welcome on-line or forms are available from most career services.

Thames Water . . . . www.twgraduaterecruitment.com
The Miller Group Ltd . . . . www.miller.co.uk
The Patent Office . . . . www.patent.gov.uk

Thames Water

www.twgraduaterecruitment.com

The Graduate Recruitment Team,
Clearwater Court, Vastern Road,
Reading, RG1 8DB
t: 0118 373 8582

Business description:
Thames Water is the UK's largest water company and the 3rd largest water company in the world. With 43 million customers in 44 countries, we cover all aspects of water business from customer service to engineering consultancy, from drinking water to treatment of waste.

N of vacancies:
We have approximately 30-40 vacancies.

Opportunities available:
Our Graduate Development Programme is designed to improve personal skills and team building. We recruit onto Mechanical, Electrical, Civil & Chemical Engineering, Finance, Human Resources and General Business Programmes.

Application procedure:
Application forms can be obtained on the web-site or by calling 0118 373 8582 for a paper version

More information about the company, our application process and our Graduate Development Programme is available on-line at www.twgraduaterecruitment.com

TRW Aeronautical Systems, Lucas Aerospace . . . .
. . . . www.trw-aeronautical.com
Whitby Bird & Partners. . . . . www.whitbybird.com

Whitby Bird & Partners

www.whitbybird.com
60 Newman Street, London, W1P 4DA,
t: 020 7631 5291

WSP Group

www.wspgroup.com
Buchanan House, 24-30 Holborn, London, EC1N 2HS
t: 020 7314 5000

Engineering > Agencies

The Graduate Recruitment Company

www.graduate-recruitment.co.uk
Alhambra House, 27-31 Charing Cross Road,
London, WC2H 0AU
t: 020 7565 3429

With moreTelecoms vacancies than any other graduate recruitment agency in the UK we are The Graduate Recruitment Agency to deal with. More Jobs, more Employers, more choices.

ASC Connections . . . . www.asc-connections.com
Better Engineers. . . . . www.betterengineers.co.uk
Calco. . . . . www.calco.co.uk
Captiva Engineering Management . . . . www.captiva-ltd.co.uk
Cummins Mellor Recruitment. . . . . www.cummins-mellor.com
Quest Technical . . . . www.quest-gb.com
Thomson-csf Support Services . . . . www.tcsf.co.uk

Engineering > Institutes

Engineering Council. . . . . www.engc.org.uk
Institute of Civil Engineers. . . . . www.ice.org.uk
Institute of Mechanical Engineers . . . . www.imeche.org.uk
Institution of Electrical Engineers . . . . www.iee.org.uk

Engineering > Motor

Ford Motor Company Ltd

www.ford.co.uk/recruitment

WWW.CHOICESONLINE.COM

Ford Motor Company Ltd . . . . www.ford.co.uk/recruitment
Honda Uk. . . . . www.autopeople.co.uk
Nissan European Technology Centre www2.nissan.co.uk

Vauxhall Motors Ltd

www.vauxhall.co.uk/graduate
info.grads@ vauxhall.co.uk

Griffin House, Osbourne Road, Luton, LU1 3YT
t: 01582 427611 **f:** 01582 426927

WWW.CHOICESONLINE.COM

Toyota Motor Manufacturing UK Ltd

www.toyota.co.uk

GraduateRecruitment@toyotauk.com

Burneston, Derbyshire, DE1 9TA
t: 01332 282 529 **f:** 01332 282803

One of the world's premiere motor brands, Toyota's commitment to the UK and Europe has made us major players in the European market. Our growth has been built on the quality of our employees and we are always interested in hearing from first class engineering graduates.

Engineering > Telecoms

Aircom International

www.aircom.co.uk

Cable & Wireless plc

www.cwplc.com

Further information: Check the websit for more details or email graduate.recruitment@cwplc.com.

Mason Communications

Mason
www.masoncom.co.uk

5 Exchange Quay, Manchester, M5 3EF
t: 0161 877 7808 **f:** 0161 877 7810

Disciplines involved: Engineering, Telecommunications, IT

Manchester (Head Office), Edinburgh, Dublin, London

Mason Communications are a telecommunications and IT consultancy providing business-orientated technology solutions

Alcatel Business Systems . . . . www.alcatel.co.uk
Cable & Wireless plc . . . . www.cwplc.com
Helios Technology . . . . www.helios-tech.co.uk
Mason Communications . . . . www.masoncom.co.uk
Motorola Ltd . . . . www.motorolacareers.com
Orange plc . . . . www.orange.co.uk
Siemens plc . . . . www.siemens.co.uk

Orange plc

www.orange.co.uk

St James Court, Great Park Rd,
Almondsbury Park, Bristol, BS32 4QJ
t: 01454 206662

Bristol and Hertford.

Disciplines available: Technical, IS, HR, marketing and finance.

Orange are a leading telecommunications company

Vodafone plc

www.vodafone.co.uk/graduates

Types of work offered: Engineering, IT, Marketing, Finance and Human Resources.

Degrees required: Any Engineering degree

N of vacancies: 50 - 100

Location: Predominantly Newbury

Application procedure: For more information, or to apply please visit our web site.

The world's leading mobile telecoms company
Vodafone set up the first analogue cellular network; introduced the first Global System for Mobile Communications (GSM); and was the first to offer text messaging and to trial WAP technology. A career with Vodafone will propel you to the forefront of one of the world's fastest growing industries.

Where graduates fit in
Our success depends not only on recruiting the most talented people, but alsoon maintaining our commitment to first-class professional development. We are looking for people with at least a 2.1 in any engineering subject to join us as engineers. And it may surprise you to hear that you don't need a technical knowledge of telecoms. It's your aptitude for learning that interests us.

What's in it for you?
Superb training, mentoring, rapid career progression, generous rewards - it's all yours when you pursue a career with Vodafone. Your personal mentor will help you navigate your way through a series of placements across the company, equipping you with a broad business overview and a wide range of specialist skills.

Vodafone plc Continued

You'll get a competitive starting salary (Masters degrees, PhDs and relevant work experience will all increase this figure) followed by about four pay reviews in the first two years.

Secure your place at the forefront and visit us at www.vodafone.co.uk/graduate

Symbian. . . . . www.symbian.com
The Graduate Recruitment Company . . . .
. . . . www.graduate-recruitment.co.uk
Vodafone plc. . . . . www.vodafone.co.uk

Food & Drink > Manufacturers

Cadbury Schweppes . . . . www.cadburyschweppes.com

Diageo plc

DIAGEO

www.diageo.com

8 Henrietta Place, London, W1G 0NB
t: 020 7927 5200 **f:** 020 7927 4600

Formed in December 1997 through the merger of GrandMet and Guinness, Diageo has an outstanding portfolio of world famous brands. These include Johnnie Walker, Guinness, Smirnoff and Tanqueray.

Together with Burger King they contribute to Diageo making occasions special every day, everywhere.

Cargill plc

www.euro.cargill.com

Kerry Group plc

www.kerrygroup.com

Thorpe Lea Manor, Thorpe Lea Road, Egham, Surrey, TW20 8HY
t: 01784 430777 **f:** 01784 470529

No of vacancies: Approximately 25

Disciplines involved: Food science, engineering, computer studies, finance and accounting, business-related or numerate degrees

Work offered: Generally in finance, IT, manufacturing, product development, quality assurance and marketing.

Application procedure: Please apply on EAF to the Graduate Recruitment Manager at the above address. For information on opportunities within Ireland, contact, the Graduate Recruitment Officer at Kerry Group plc, Princess Street, trainee, Co Kerry, Ireland.

Kerry Group plc is an international food ingredients corporation with interests in Ireland, the UK, Europe, the USA, Canada, South America, Malaysia and Australia. As Ireland's leading food processing business, Kerry employs 5,500 in the UK and over 12,5000 world-wide.

Nestlé UK Ltd

www.nestlegrad.co.uk

Northern Foods plc

www.northern-foods.co.uk

Geest plc . . . . www.geest.co.uk
Kerry Group plc . . . . www.kerrygroup.com
Kraft Foods UK Ltd. . . . . www.kraft.com
Nestl UK Ltd . . . . www.nestlegrad.co.uk
Northern Foods plc . . . . www.northern-foods.co.uk
Science Recruitment Group . . . . www.srg.co.uk
Scottish & Newcastle plc . . . . www.scottish-newcastle.com
Tate & Lyle . . . . www.tate-lyle.co.uk
Walkers Snack Ltd . . . . www.walkers.co.uk
Whitbread plc. . . . . www.whitbread.com

Science Recruitment Group

www.srg.co.uk

Buckland House, Langley Business Park,
Slough, Berks, SL3 6EZ
t: 01753 589700

For contract, permanent and senior management positions within science based industries.

Freight & Logistics

Argos Ltd . . . . www.argos.co.uk

CERT Group of Companies plc.

www.cert.co.uk
info@cert.co.uk
careers@cert.co.uk

Bruce Way,, Whetstone, Leicester, LE8 6YG
t: 0116 2750808 **f:** 0116 2750752

Maersk

www.maersk.co.uk

P & O Nedlloyd Ltd

P&O Nedlloyd

www.ponl.com

Beagle House, Braham Street, London, E1 8EP
t: 020 7441 1000

N of vacancies: Up to 4 vacancies.

Disciplines involved: Any although business related qualifications will prove useful.

Recruited to: Management trainees

P & O Nedlloyd Ltd is at the forefront of international freight transport industry, offering a worldwide, door to door container service by land and sea. P & O Nedlloyd holds leading positions in the Atlantic and Europe/Asia trades, and the most comprehensive presence in north/south trades worldwide. We have a worldwide employee number of 10,500.

Safeway Stores plc

www.safeway.co.uk

Safeway House, 6 Millington Road,
Hayes, Middlesex, UB3 4AY
t: 0800 269 718

No of vacancies: Approx. 20 vacancies.

Disciplines involved: We welcome applicants from any degree discipline (minimum of 2:2).

Training: Our unique training programme incorporates Safeway specific skills along with management skills and an opportunity to study for the Institute of Grocery Distribution Postgraduate Diploma.

Types of work offered: Opportunities on the Safeway Graduate Programme exist in our three main divisions: Retail Operations, Distribution or Store Support Centre (including trading, marketing, logistics, property development, supply chain and human resources).

Salary: Starting salary around ú18,400.

Safeway stores plc is one of top four food retailers, employing in excess of 85,000 people, with an annual turnover of ú9 billion. Our nationwide portfolio of almost 500 stores offers the widest geographical spread of any of the main UK food retailers.

WWW.CHOICESONLINE.COM

Consignia

www.consignia.co.uk

Coton House Management Center,
Coton House, Rugby, CV23 0AA
t: 020 7239 2000

United Parcel Service Ltd.

www.ups.co.uk

Forest Road, Feltham, Middlesex, TW13 7DY

TNT UK Ltd . . . . www.tnt.co.uk
Toys "R" Us . . . . www.toysrus.co.uk
United Parcel Service Ltd. . . . . www.ups.co.uk
Wincanton Logistics . . . . www.wincanton.co.uk

Hospitality & Leisure

Blitz Games . . . . www.BlitzGames.com

Bourne Leisure Ltd

www.havenholidays.com
www.butlins.co.uk
www.british-holidays.co.uk
www.warnerholidays.co.uk
www.oasisholidays.co.uk
www.haveneurope.co.uk

Blitz Games

www.BlitzGames.com

PO Box 186, Leamington Spa,
Warwickshire, CV32 5TX
t: 01926 311 284   **f:** 01926 887 209

Business description: Blitz Games is an independent games development company established in 1991. Over 100 professional and dedicated employees work in a friendly, young and well structured environment.

N of vacancies: Check web-site for latest vacancies.

Application procedure: Application forms are available on our web-site or alternatively, you can send us a full and up-to-date CV along with a covering letter to the above address. Please remember to enclose a demo of your work (your application will be reviewed quicker). More information on breaking into the Computer Games industry is available on our web-site www.BlitzGames.com

Bourne Leisure Ltd . . . . birmingham@pps500.co.uk
Compass Group Uk . . . . www.compass-group.co.uk
De Vere Hotels . . . . www.devere.co.uk
Eidos Interactive Ltd . . . . www.eidos.co.uk
McDonald's Restaurants Ltd . . . . www.mcdonalds.co.uk
Moto Hospitality Ltd . . . . www.moto-way.com

Moto Hospitality Ltd

www.moto-way.com

De Vere Hotels

DE VERE HOTELS

Hotels of character, run with pride

www.devere.co.uk

Wilderspool House, Greenalls Avenue, Warrington,
Cheshire, WA4 6RH
t: 01928 756 155 **f:** 01928 756 341

More company information is available on our web-site at:
www.ybs.co.uk

De Vere Group Plc is a highly focused company concentrating on
two growth markets - hotels and health & fitness. The company
has two distinctive and expanding hotel brands; De Vere Hotels
and Village Leisure Hotels, and a rapidly growing standalone
health & fitness brand - Greens.

Institutes and Associations

Association of Accounting Technicians . . . . www.aat.co.uk
Association of Chartered Certified Accountants . . . .
. . . . www.accaglobal.com
Association of Corporate Treasurers . . . . www.treasurers.org
British Pharmacological Society . . . . www.bps.ac.uk
Chartered Institute of Building. . . . . www.ciob.org.uk
Chartered Institute of Management Accountants . . www.cima.org.uk
Chartered Institute of Personnel and Development (CIPD) . . . . .
. . . . www.cipd.co.uk
Chartered Institute of Purchasing & Supply . . . . www.cips.org
Engineering Council. . . . . www.engc.org.uk
European Commission. www.europa.eu.int

Association of Chartered Certified Accountants

www.accaglobal.com

29 Lincoln's Inn Fields, London, WC2A 3EE
t: 020 7396 5800 **f:** 020 7396 5858

The Association of Chartered Certified Accountants (ACCA) has been recognised and respected across the world for almost 100 years, and currently has nearly 300,000 students and members in 160 countries.

The ACCA qualification is a highly relevant, targeted combination of study and practical experience, and is widely recognised in all sectors throughout the world.

Chartered Institute of Building

www.ciob.org.uk

Englemere, Kings Ride, Ascot, Berkshire, SL5 8BJ
t: 01344 630 700 **f:** 01344 630 777

The Chartered Institute of Building is the professional body for today's managers in construction.

The Institute has almost 40,000 members, skilled managers and professionals drawn from the top ranks of the construction industry, with a common commitment to achieve and maintain the highest possible standards.

Chartered Institute of Personnel and Development (CIPD)

www.cipd.co.uk

CIPD House, Camp Road, London, SW19 4UX
t: 020 8971 9000 **f:** 020 8263 3333

The Chartered Institute of Personnel and Development (CIPD) is Europe's largest professional institute for all those concerned with people management and development. The CIPD has 110,000 members and sets standards for professionals in the field. Grades of membership are determined by qualifications and attained experience, membership is highly respected and widely accepted by employers as requirements of practice.

The Institute of Chartered Accountants of Scotland

www.icas.org.uk

CA House, 21 Haymarket Yards, Edinburgh, EH12 5BH
t: 0131 347 0161 **f:** 0131 349 0108

Faculty & Institute of Actuaries . . . . www.actuaries.org.uk
Institute of Careers Guidance . . . . www.icg-uk.org

Institute of Careers Guidance

www.icg-uk.org

Insurance & Finance - Employers

AA Insurance . . . . www.theaa.co.uk
Allied Dunbar Assurance plc . . . . www.allieddunbar.co.uk
Barclays Life Assurance Company Ltd . . . . www.life.barclays.co.uk
Benfield Grieg Group . . . . www.benfieldgrieg.com

Harrison-Beaumont

www.hbinsurance.co.uk

BIIBA . . . . www.biiba.org.uk
Co-operative Insurance Society Ltd . . . . www.cis.co.uk
Cornhill Insurance plc . . . . www.cornhill.co.uk
Fox-Pitt, Kelton. . . . . www.fpk.com

JLT Risk Solutions Ltd

JARDINE LLOYD THOMPSON
Group plc

www.jltgroup.com

6 Crutched Friars, London, EC3N 2PH
t: 020 7528 4000 **f:** 020 7528 4500

Disciplines involved: Any Degree.

Types of work offered: Administration and Management;
Finance; Insurance Brokers

Online application available.

JLT is a leading international provider of risk solution and
insurance services. JLT employs over 4,000 people worldwide
in over 100 offices in 35 countries.

Scottish Life

www.scottishlife.co.uk

19 St. Andrew Square, Edinburgh, EH2 1YE
t: 0131 456 7777

Scottish Life is a marketing division of the Royal London Group, one of the strongest financial services groups in the UK.

Taylor Nelson Sofres

www.tnsofres.com

Harrison-Beaumont . . . . www.hbinsurance.co.uk
Jardine Lloyd Thompson . . . . www.jltgroup.com
JLT Risk Solutions Ltd . . . . www.jltgroup.com
Liverpool Victoria . . . . www.liverpool-victoria.co.uk
Lloyds of London . . . . www.lloyds.com
Prudential Corporation plc . . . . www.prudential.co.uk
Scottish Life . . . . www.scottishlife.co.uk
Standard Life Assurance Company . . . . www.individuals.co.uk
Swinton Group Ltd . . . . www.swinton.co.uk
Taylor Nelson Sofres . . . . www.tnsofres.com
William M. Mercer Ltd. . . . . www.wmmercer.com
Willis Group Ltd . . . . www.willis.com

International

Abatec International . . . . www.abatec.co.uk
ALSTOM UK Ltd. . . . . www.alstom.com

Citigroup Corporate & Investment Bank/Schroder Salomon Smith Barney

www.citigroup.com/newgrads/recruits

33 Canada Square, Canary Wharf, London, E14 5LB
t: 020 7986 5309

Minimum required: Graduate level entry positions require a minimum 2:1 or equivalent. Any degree subject considered.

Application procedure: On-line application system via website.

Closing date: For full time applications, 30th November. For Summer Internship applications 28th February 2002.

Citigroup are a CORPORATE INVESTMENT BANK and the 3rd largest public finance company in the world.

WWW.CHOICESONLINE.COM

Bechtel Ltd. . . . . www.bechtel.co.uk
Cadbury Schweppes . . . . www.cadburyschweppes.com
Cap Gemini Ernst & Young. . . . . www.uk.cgey.co.uk
Citigroup Corporate & Investment Bank/Schroder Salomon Smith Barney . . . .
. . . . www.citigroup.com
Clarks International . . . . www.clarks.com
Dixon Wilson. . . . . www.dixonwilson.com
DLA . . . . www.dla.com
F.I.Group PLC . . . . www.figroup.co.uk
Gouldens . . . . www.gouldens.com
Herbert Smith . . . . www.herbertsmith.com
HSBC . . . . www.hsbc.com/recruitment
IMI . . . . www.imi.plc.uk

Herbert Smith

HERBERT SMITH

www.herbertsmith.com

Exchange House, Primrose Street, London, EC2A 2HS
t: 020 7374 8000

Herbert Smith is an international law firm with offices throughout Europe and Asia. Our 3 main divisions are Corporate, Finance and Dispute Resolution. As well as these we offer a range of specialist services across 6 additional departments.

Graduate Recruitment
We recruit graduates every March and September and take on around 90 trainees a year.

Training
We offer a 2 year training scheme compromising of 4 seats. Trainees preferences are taken into account and there may be an opportunity to spend a seat in one of our international offices or a client secondment.

Vacation Schemes
Vacation schemes are open to students from all disciplines. They run at Christmas, Easter and during the summer with about 90 places in total.

Apply
We recruit our trainees from all disciplines. All applications should b made on-line.

WWW.CHOICESONLINE.COM

ING Barings	www.ingbarings.com/careers
KPMG	www.kpmgcareers.co.uk
Lehman Brothers	www.lehman.com
Mars	www.mars.com/university
Merrill Lynch & Co	www.ml.com/careers
Nabarro Nathanson	www.nabarro.com

Mars

www.mars.com/university
mars.graduate@eu.effem.com

Graduate Marketing,
Dundee Road, Slough,
Berks, SL1 4JX
t: 017 5351 4999

Working at Mars is different. From day 1 we offer unrivalled stimulation, challenge and opportunity to high calibre graduates.

N of vacancies: Mars Management Training Programme - 20-25 Other Programmes - 15-20

Disciplines involved: MMTP - Any disciplines

Opportunities available: MMTP - Sales, marketing, production manufacturing, research & development, engineering, commercial, logistics, finance, personnel. Functional Programmes - Finance, Engineering, Software Engineering, IT

Locations: Thames Valley, Leeds, Leicestershire.
Hotline: 017 5351 4999

Mars Incorporated is a world leader in each of its main businesses: branded snack foods, petcare products, main meal foods, automated payment systems and drinks vending. We are a truly international business with over 140 sites in more than 60 countries worldwide and have an annual turnover in excess of \$13 billion.

Shell

www.shell.com
www.shell.com/careers
Response@si.shell.com

Rowlandsway House, Rowlandsway, Manchester, M22 5SB
t: 0845 600 1819 **f:** 0161 499 4859

N of vacancies: We have approximately 500 graduate vacancies worldwide.

Disciplines involved: Any discipline will be considered although for Technical vacancies a relevant degree subject is required.

Type of work offered: Engineering, Finance, Marketing and Sales, Supply Chain, Information Technology, eBusiness, Human Resources, Trading and Research.

Locations: Over 120 countries worldwide.

Application procedure: For an application form visit our website or telephone 0845 600 1819.

Shell is at the heart of the energy and petrochemical business, and one of the world's most successful organisations. Our business is unique. It not only has a huge impact on global development, but also offers international career prospects and outstanding challenges.

Science Recruitment Group

www.srg.co.uk

Buckland House, Langley Business Park,
Slough, Berks, SL3 6EZ
t: 01753 589700

For contract, permanent and senior management positions within science based industries.

Syntegra Ltd

www.syntegra.com
graduaterecruit@syntegra.com

Guidion House, Harvest Crescent,
Ancells Business Park,
Fleet, Hampshire, GU151 2QP
t: 01635 584135

N of vacancies: 40 worldwide.

Disciplines involved: Any discipline considered. Business and IT- related subjects of particular interest.   Strong record of academic achievement is essential.

Opportunities: For a business or technology focussed career - visit our website for more information.

Locations: Fleet, Leeds, Newcastle but mobility required as projects could be based at other locations in the UK, mainland Europe, US or S.E Asia

Application procedure: For an application form, call our graduate hotline on 01635 584135 or visit our website above.

The consultancy and systems integration business of BT, Syntegra is a major global business with customers in more than 50 countries. Syntegra is a major player in the e-business revolution, transforming the performance of customers in a range of markets through the creative application of advanced technology.

VSO

www.vso.org.uk

317 Putney Bridge Road, London, SW15 2PN

Types of work offered: Teaching placements for recent graduates and other placements in education, IT, health, business, social and community work, engineering and technical professions for those with relevant experience.

N of vacancies: 200 graduate placements a year out of 1,000 total placements.

Opportunities available: The chance to share skills with local communities in over 50 developing countries worldwide, make lasting friendships and return enriched personally and professionally by the experience.

Support from VSO: Quality training and support, return airfares, medical cover, salary, benefit payments, grants.

Further information: Website: for placement information and events. Email enquiry@vso.org.uk. Ring someone who's been there and done it: 0845 603 0027 or our Enquiry unit on 020 8780 7500, mini-com 020 8780 7440.

InternetSites

WCN (World Careers Network)

www.wcn.co.uk

The World's Careers Network has an international website with a strong European focus offering outstanding careers advice.

Particularly informative for under graduates and finalists, it offers details of full-time vacancies, placements, vacation work and internships..

Registration means that suitable job vacancies can be emailed to you free of charge.

Milkround . . . . www.milkround.co.uk
Prospects Web . . . . www.prospects.csu.ac.uk
Real World Magazine . . . . www.realworldmagazine.com
Science Recruitment Group . . . . www.srg.co.uk
Top Grads . . . . www.topgrads.co.uk
WCN (World Careers Network) . . . . www.wcn.co.uk

IT > Agencies

Job Loop . . . . www.jobloop.com
JobServe . . . . www.jobserve.com
The Graduate Recruitment Company . . . .
. . . . www.graduate-recruitment.co.uk

Job Loop

www.jobloop.com

IT > Employers

Aerosystems International . . . . www.aeroint.com

Aerosystems International

www.aeroint.com

WWW.CHOICESONLINE.COM

BOC

www.bocgrads.co.uk

WWW.CHOICESONLINE.COM

GCHQ

www.gchq.gov.uk

WWW.CHOICESONLINE.COM

Alenia Marconi Systems

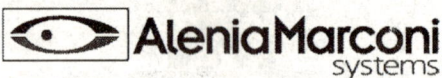

www.aleniamarconisystems.com
isd.recruitment@amsjv.com

Lyon Way, Frimley Road,
Camberley, Surrey, GU16 5EX
t: 01276 63311

Have you ever wondered how a missile reaches it's target or how planes fly safely through the sky? Are you an Engineer interested in working at the cutting edge of the defence and electronics industry?

If the answer is yes, Alenia Marconi may have an opportunity for you. We are looking for Software, Hardware and System Engineers to join a world leader in the provision of integrated defence and electronic systems solutions.

With a customer base in over 100 countries, we are acknowledged experts in ground and naval radar, missile systems, air traffic management, command and control, simulation and synthetic environments, engineering, software design and manufacturing.

IBM (United Kindom) Limited

www.ibm.com/employment/europe/graduate
3grad@uk.ibm.com

The Graduate Recruitment Team, North Harbour,
Portsmouth, Hampshire, PO6 3AU
t: 023 9256 4015

Intel

www.intel.com/jobs

Pipers Way, Swindon, SN3 1RJ

Nokia

www.nokia.co.uk/careers

Alenia Marconi Systems . . . . www.aleniamarconisystems.com
BOC . . . . www.bocgrads.co.uk
GCHQ . . . . www.gchq.gov.uk
IBM (United Kindom) Limited . . . .
. . . . www.ibm.com/employment/europe/graduate
IMI . . . . www.imi.plc.uk
Intel. . . . . www.intel.com/jobs
Keane Ltd . . . . www.keane.uk.com

Orange plc

www.orange.co.uk

St James Court, Great Park Rd, Almondsbury Park,
Bristol, BS32 4QJ
t: 01454 206662

Bristol and Hertford.

Disciplines available: Technical, IS, HR, marketing and finance.

Orange are a leading telecommunications company

Reuters plc

REUTERS :)

www.reuters.com/careers/graduate
ukgraduate.recruitment@reuters.com

85 Fleet St, London, EC4P 4AJ

Vodafone plc

vodafone

www.vodafone.co.uk/graduates

Types of work offered: Engineering, IT, Marketing, Finance and Human Resources.

Degrees required: You must have at least a 2.1. To join us as an Engineer, your degree must be in Engineering or a related subject; however, IT, HR, Finance and Marketing are open to graduates from more or varied disciplines.

N of vacancies: c25

Location: Predominantly Newbury.

The world's leading mobile telecoms company:
Vodafone set up the first analogue cellular network; introduced the first Global System for Mobile Communications (GSM); and was the first to offer text messaging and to trial WAP technology. A career with Vodafone will propel you to the forefront of one of the world's fastest growing industries.

Vodafone plc Continued

Where graduates fit in:
Our success depends not only on recruiting the most talented people, but also on maintaining our commitment to first-class professional development. We are looking for people with at least a 2.1 in any subject to join us in IT. And it may surprise you to hear that you don't need a technical knowledge of telecoms. It's your aptitude for learning that interests us.

What's in it for you:
Superb training, mentoring, rapid career progression, generous rewards - it's all yours when you pursue a career with Vodafone. Your personal mentor will help you navigate your way through a series of placements across the company, equipping you with a broad business overview and a wide range of specialist skills.

You'll get a competitive starting salary (Masters degrees, PhDs and relevant work experience will all increase this figure) followed by about four pay reviews in the first two years.

Secure your place at the forefront and visit us at www.vodafone.co.uk/graduates

IT > Software Houses

Acxiom

www.acxiom.com

Aircom International

www.aircom.co.uk

Altera Europe

www.altera.com

Holmers Farm Way, High Wycombe,
Buckinghamshire, HP12 4XF
t: 01494 602000

ARM

www.arm.com

110 Fulbourn Road, Cambridge, CB1 9NJ
t: 01223 400400

Altera Europe . . . . www.altera.com
ARM . . . . www.arm.com
Cap Gemini Ernst & Young . . . . www.uk.cgey.co.uk
CMG plc . . . . www.cmg.co.uk
Computer Sciences Corporation . . . . www.csc.com
Cramer Systems Ltd . . . . www.cramersystems.com

Cyberscience plc

www.cyberscience.com

Rawdon House, High Street,
Hoddesdon, Hertfordshire, EN11 8BD
t: 01992 411 111

CMG plc

www.cmg.co.uk
graduate@cmgplc.com

Parnell House, 25 Wilton Rd, London, SW1V 1EJ
t: 0500 516 151

CMG plc is a global Information and Communications Technology group providing business information solutions through consultancy, systems and services.

With headquarters in London and Hoofddorp (near Amsterdam), CMG now implements and supports applications for customers worldwide from bases in 16 countries.

Recruitment
We are now looking for IT oriented graduates who have, or are expecting, a 2:1 in any numerate scientific degree, and have some programming experience. Vacancies are advertised on-line with details of application dates and requirements.

Applying
Application forms can be found on-line or forward a CV to graduate@cmgplc.com or post to the address above.

Detica

www.detica.com

Surrey Research Park, Guildford, GU2 7YP
t: 01483 442 2022

Data Connection Ltd

www.dataconnection.com
recruit@dataconnection.com

100 Church Street, Enfield, Middlesex, EN2 6BQ
t: 020 8366 1177 **f:** 020 8363 2927

DVA

www.dva.co.uk

I-teba

www.iteba.com

IPL

www.iplbath.com
jobs@iplbath.com

Logica

www.logica.com
www.logica.com/ukgraduates

The Graduate Recruitment Office,
Freepost 21, London, W1E 4JZ
t: 0845 120 0294

Disciplines involved: Computer science, mathematics, physics, engineering or any numerate/logical discipline. Candidates studying business related degrees with excellent academic records and a keen interest in computing will also be considered

N of vacancies: Approx. 350

Contact name: Mark Donmall

Locations: London, Surrey, Brentwood, Reading, Slough, Bristol, Manchester, West Midlands, Cambridge, Edinburgh and Aberdeen.

Milkround visits: Please see our websites for details of our presentation programme.

Logica is one of the leading IT companies. We are in business to help leading organisations world wide achieve their business objectives through the innovative use of IT.

Lynx Financial Systems

www.lynx-fs.com

Oaklands Manor, Thorner Lane, Scarcroft, Leeds, LS14 3AH

Microgen-Kaisha

www.microgen.co.uk

Milford House, Milford Street, Swindon, Wiltshire, SN1 1DW
t: 01793 480048

Micromuse . . . . www.micromuse.com
Midas-Kapiti International . . . . www.midas-kapiti.com
Misys plc . . . . www.midas-kapiti.com
NCC . . . . www.nccglobal.com
Oracle Corporation UK Ltd . . . . jobs.oracle.com/graduates

Micromuse

www.micromuse.com

Disraeli House, 90 Putney Bridge Road, London, SW18 1DA
t: 020 8875 9500

London (EMEA Office)

Have fun. Get paid. How cool is that? At Micromuse, you'll be part of the 8th fastest growing IT company in the world according to Business Week.

We produce Netcool, the world's leading service level management software. And even more importantly, Netcool's core development happens right here in London. So there's no hanging around waiting to get involved with the important stuff. What are you waiting for?

Oracle Corporation UK Ltd

jobs.oracle.com/graduates

Recruitment Dept, Oracle Parkway, Thames Valley Park,
Reading, Berks, RG6 1RA
t: 0118 924 5572

Subjects of study: IT related degree. Ideally 2:1 or above.

Work offered: Consulting, Product development
(designer/developer 2000 and applications).

Locations: Reading and Hemel Hempstead

Application is through the website only.

Oracle are a leading supplier of software information, technology
services and solutions.

PA Consulting Group

www.paconsulting.com

PA Consulting Group . . . . www.paconsulting.com
Parity Solutions Ltd . . . . www.parity-solutions.co.uk
Perot Systems Corporation . . . . www.perotsystems.com
PinkRoccade . . . . www.pinkroccade.com
RM plc. . . . . www.rm.com

PinkRoccade

www.pinkroccade.com

Rolfe & Nolan

www.rolfeandnolen.com

Lowndes House, 1-9 City Road, London, EC1Y 1AE
t: 020 7374 4841

Rolfe & Nolan is a financial software house specialising in the development of derivatives and treasury products for the futures and options industry.

Sanderson Group plc

www.sanderson.com

2115 Coventry Road, Sheldon, Birmingham, B26 3EA
t: 0121 359 4861

Sanderson is a forward thinking international IT Group.

Systems Mechanics Ltd

www.sysmech.co.uk

65/67 High Street, Whitstable, Kent, CT5 1AP
t: 01227 773 000

Established in 1993, Systems Mechanics develop Network Management Software Solutions for the Telecommunications industry.

CV's can be sent to graduates@sysmech.co.uk and further details of vacancies can be found on the website.

Syntegra Ltd

www.syntegra.com

graduaterecruit@syntegra.com

Guidion House, Harvest Crescent, Ancells Business Park,
Fleet, Hampshire, GU51 2QP
t: 01635 584135

N of vacancies: 40 worldwide.

Disciplines involved: Any discipline considered. Business and IT- related subjects of particular interest. Strong record of academic achievement is essential.

Opportunities: For a business or technology focussed career - visit our website for more information.

Locations: Fleet, Leeds, Newcastle but mobility required as projects could be based at other locations in the UK, mainland Europe, US or S.E Asia

Application procedure: For an application form, call our graduate hotline on 01635 584135 or visit our website above.

The consultancy and systems integration business of BT, Syntegra is a major global business with customers in more than 50 countries. Syntegra is a major player in the e-business revolution, transforming the performance of customers in a range of markets through the creative application of advanced technology.

Scorex UK Ltd

www.scorex.com

Sanderson Group plc	www.sanderson.com
Science Systems	www.scisys.co.uk
Scorex UK Ltd	www.scorex.com
Syntegra Ltd	www.syntegra.com
Systems Mechanics Ltd	www.sysmech.co.uk
Urban Science International Ltd	www.urbanscience.com

Urban Science International Ltd

www.urbanscience.com

Urban Science House, Gogmore Lane, Chertsey, Surrey,
KT16 9AP
t: 01932 574 400

Urban Science is one of the world's largest Automotive Consulting firms. IT consultancy roles available throughout Europe.

Applications to: SMBowers@urbanscience.com

Job Fairs

Accountancy Career Fair	www.londoncareers.net
Careers & Jobs Live	www.jarvis-exhibitions.com
Finance Fair	www.careers.ox.ac.uk

Careers & Jobs Live

www.jarvis-exhibitions.com

Jarvis Exhibitions

www.jarvis-exhibitions.com
Careers & Jobs Live
Spring & Autumn Graduate Recruitment Fairs
Scottish Graduate Recruitment Fairs

t: 020 8464 4129 **f:** 020 8466 5970

Jarvis Exhibitions are the UK's premiere recruitment event organiser. For face to face contact with more graduate recruiters than ever before visit our web site and fix a date in your diary to join us in London, Manchester, Birmingham or Glasgow.

WWW.CHOICESONLINE.COM

Job Scene

Job Scene

www.jobsceneuk.co.uk

A TJW Exhibition

WWW.CHOICESONLINE.COM

Science Recruitment Group

www.srg.co.uk

Buckland House, Langley Business Park,
Slough, Berks, SL3 6EZ
t: 01753 589700

For contract, permanent and senior management positions within
science based industries.

Scottish Graduate Recruitment Fair

www.jarvis-exhibitions.com

Spring & Autumn Graduate Recruitment Fairs

www.jarvis-exhibitions.com

Lawyers

Abel & Imray. 020 7405 0203
Addleshaw Booth & Co . . . . www.addleshaw-booth.co.uk
Allen & Overy . . . . www.allenovery.com
Ashurst Morris Crisp. . . . . www.ashursts.com
Baker & McKenzie . . . . www.ukgraduates.bakernet.com

---

Ashurst Morris Crisp

www.ashursts.com
gradrec@ashursts.com

Broadwalk House, 5 Appold Street, London, EC2A 2HA
t: 020 7972 7000 **f:** 020 7972 7800

Minimum degree required: 2:1 or higher, to be supported by high achievements outside academic matters.

Salaries: Starting at ú28,000 .

Application procedure: On-line.

Find out more: Brochures regarding Graduate Recruitment available on-line.

Ashurst Morris Crisp is a law firm with offices in London, Frankfurt, New Delhi, Singapore, Tokyo, New York, Milan, Brussels and Paris. A corporate law practice specialising in finance, commercial & banking law, property & planning, litigation, employment and tax. Every year we seek to recruit a number of graduates who want to be involved in the highest quality national, international and multi-national work that City firms can offer. A copy of our online Graduate Recruitment brochure is available from our website.

Allen & Overy

ALLEN & OVERY

www.allenovery.com

graduate.recruitment@allenovery.com

One New Change, London, EC4M 9QQ

t: 020 7330 3000

Locations

Amsterdam, Antwerp, Bangkok, Beijing, Bratislava, Brussels, Budapest, Dubai, Frankfurt, Hamburg, Hong Kong, London, Luxembourg, Madrid, Milan, Moscow, New York, Paris, Prague, Rome, Singapore, Tirana, Tokyo, Turin and Warsaw.

About Allen & Overy

Allen & Overy is one of the world's premier law firms, with an international reputation for serving multinational businesses, financial institutions, governments and private individuals wherever there is a need for decisive legal advice on complex transactions. We have international expertise in the fields of banking, corporate and international capital markets. Independent legal directories rank us first or equal in many areas, including lending, civil fraud, derivatives, environmental, financial services regulation, insolvency, international capital markets, partnership law, project finance, securitisations, trusts and personal tax and VAT.

WWW.CHOICESONLINE.COM

Abel & Imray

020 7405 0203

20 Red Lion Street, London, WC1R 4PQ

t: 020 7405 0203

London (Head Office), Bath, Cardiff, Munich. Abel & Imray are a firm of Patent Attorneys and Trade Mark Attorneys

WWW.CHOICESONLINE.COM

Baker & McKenzie

www.ukgraduates.bakernet.com

100 New Bridge Street, London, EC4V 6JA
t: 020 7919 1000 **f:** 020 7919 1258

Disciplines involved: Law

Baker & McKenzie is the law firm with the greatest global reach, with 62 offices in 35 countries.

For more details contact the Graduate Recruitment Department on the telephone number above or visit our graduate website.

Bond Pearce

www.bondpearce.com
trainees@bondpearce.com

Bond Pearce's merger with Cartwrights consolidates its position as one of the UK's leading law firms with over 60 Partners and a total staff in excess of 600. We are also one of the fastest growing firms with a network of offices from Plymouth to London, and Leeds to Southampton.

Application procedure: For a trainee brochure and EAF please contact Krishna Anand on T: 0117 929 9197, F: 0117 926 2403

Clyde & Co

CLYDE&CO
INTERNATIONAL LAW FIRM
www.clydeco.com

51 Eastcheap, London, EC3M 1JP
t: 020 7623 1244

London, Guildford, Cardiff.

Contact name: Georgia de Saram - Graduate Recruitment Manager

Graduate recruitment hotline: 020 7648 1580

Number of Training Contracts offered each year: 20

Disciplines in: Law

Clyde & Co is an international law firm with regional offices in Europe, the Middle East, the Far East and Latin America. Mainly dealing with trade, shipping, transport, insurance, reinsurance, corporate and financial matters.

CMS Cameron McKenna

CMS Cameron McKenna

www.cmck.com/gradrec

Mitre House, 160 Aldersgate Street, London, EC1A 4DD
t: 020 7367 2842

Disciplines involved: Law

CMS Cameron McKenna are an international law firm with six main areas of practice: Banking; Corporate; Insurance; Property; Commercial; and Energy, Projects and Construction.

Denton Wilde Sapte

www.dentonwildesapte.com

5 Chancery lane, Clifford's Inn, London, EC4A 1BC
t: 020 7242 1212

A truly international firm, strong in Europe, the CIS, the Middle East and Asia. Founder Members of Denton International, a network of leading law firms.

The main areas of expertise are Banking and Finance, Corporate, Energy, Technology, Media, Telecommunications, Litigation and Property.

WWW.CHOICESONLINE.COM

Institute of Legal Executives

www.ilex.org.uk
jburns@ilex.org.uk

Kempston Manor, Kempston, Bedford, MK42 7AB
t: 01234 841 000 f: 01234 841 999

A professional body representing over 22,000 legal executives and trainee legal executives.

WWW.CHOICESONLINE.COM

Clifford Chance . . . . www.cliffordchance.com
Clyde & Co . . . . www.clydeco.com

Legal Services Commission

www.legalservices.gov.uk

WWW.CHOICESONLINE.COM

Linklaters & Alliance

LINKLATERS & ALLIANCE

www.linklaters.com/recruitment

graduate.recruitment@linklaters.com

One Silk Street, London, EC2Y 8HQ

Head Office in London + 34 overseas offices

Discipline Required: Any

Linklaters & Alliance are a large global law firm with three main areas of practice; corporate, global finance & projects and specialist areas.

Mills & Reeve

www.mills-reeve.com

Francis House, 112 Hills Road, Cambridge, CB2 1PH
t: 01223 364422 **f:** 01223 222319

Mills & Reeve is one of the U's largest law firms, with 60 partners and over 250 lawyers operating throughout the country from offices in Birmingham, Cambridge, London and Norwich.

We offer a full range of corporate, commercial, property, litigation and private client services and are national specialists in the technology, education, healthcare, insurance and land and agricultural sectors.

Around 20 - 25 trainees are taken on each year and a list of current vacancies can be found on the website. Alternatively, for a full brochure and application form contact Graduate Recruitment on the number above.

Macfarlanes

MACFARLANES

www.macfarlanes.com

10 Norwich Street, London, EC4A 1BD
t: 020 7831 9222

Macfarlanes is a City law firm, widely recognised as one of a handful of high quality, unaligned law firms in the UK. Core practice areas include corporate; property; litigation and private client.

Graduate recruitment
Macfarlanes takes on around 25 graduate trainees each year and offers around 40 summer placements. Any degree discipline will be considered as successful applicants will spend 2 years training.

Training
The 2 year training contract combines hands on experience with a first class education and training programme. This includes departmental seminars, workshops, legal update meetings and regular trainee workshops.

Further information
An application form can be downloaded or requested on-line. Any other enquiries should be directed to Graham Stoddart at gs@macfarlanes.com.

CMS Cameron McKenna . . . . www.cmck.com/gradrec
Coudert Brothers . . . . www.coudert.com
Denton Wilde Sapte . . . . www.dentonwildesapte.com
DLA . . . . www.dla.com
Dundas & Wilson . . . . www.dundas-wilson.com
Field Fisher Waterhouse . . . . www.ffwlaw.com

Martineau Johnson

MARTINEAU JOHNSON

www.martineau-johnson.co.uk
www.graduates4law.com
emily.dean@martjohn.com

St Philips House, St Philips Place, Birmingham, West
Midlands, B3 2PP
t: 0121 200 3300
f: 0121 633 7433

Martineau Johnson is a leading law firm with offices in
Birmingham and London.

N of vacancies
We take on 14 graduate trainee solicitors each September.

Requirements
You will have a good degree grade - not necessarily in law.

Training
Our trainee solicitors enjoy a full and varied programme involving
seats of 4 months instead of 6 months. This gives trainees
maximum flexibility and choice.

Further information
Apply on-line: graduates4law.com or by paper application form
from Emily Dean.

Gouldens . . . . www.gouldens.com
Hammond Suddards Edge . . . . . www.hammondsuddardsedge.com
Herbert Smith . . . . www.herbertsmith.com
Holman Fenwick & Willan . . . . www.holmanfenwick.com
Institute of Legal Executives . . . . www.ilex.org.uk
Lawrence Graham . . . . www.lawgram.com
Legal Services Commission . . . . www.legalservices.gov.uk

Norton Rose

www.nortonrose.com

Kempson House, Camomile Street,
London, EC3A 7AN
t: 020 7283 6000

Athens*, Bahrain, Bangkok, Brussels, Cologne, Frankfurt, Jakarta*, London, Milan, Moscow, Munich, Paris, Pireaus*, Singapore, Warsaw. * Associate Office

Disciplines involved: Law

Types of work offered: commercial/company, banking/finance, aviation, commercial litigation, commercial property and planning, taxation, marine litigation, intellectual property and technology, competition and EC, employment, pensions and incentives.

Norton Rose are a large corporate and commercial law firm with a strong international practice.

Linklaters & Alliance . . . . www.linklaters.com/recruitment
Macfarlanes . . . . www.macfarlanes.com
Martineau Johnson . . . . www.martineau-johnson.co.uk
Masons . . . . www.masons.com
Mills & Reeve . . . . www.mills-reeve.com
Morgan Cole . . . . www.morgan-cole.com
Nabarro Nathanson . . . . www.nabarro.com
Nicholson Graham & Jones . . . . www.ngj.co.uk
Norton Rose . . . . www.nortonrose.com
Olswang . . . . www.olswang.com
Osborne Clark . . . . www.osborneclark.com
Pannone & Partners Solicitors . . . . www.pannone.com

Olswang

OLSWANG

www.olswang.com

90 Long Acre, London, WC2E 9TT
t: 020 7208 8888 **f:** 020 7208 8800

Olswang is a specialist law firm providing a full range of legal services to clients in the technology, media and telecommunication sectors. We have a staff of over 450 employees and offices in London and Brussels.

Graduates
We take on up to 25 graduates a year as trainee solicitors. Applications by CV and covering letter to James Hacking by 29th July 2002.

Requirements
We require all applicants to have good A-level grades and a 2:1 degree. We recruit our trainees from any degree discipline.

Summer placements
We run three two week placements during the summer. To apply send a CV and covering letter to James Hacking by 1st March 2002.

Professional qualifications
We pay all fees and a maintenance grant for successful candidates taking the Legal Practice Course (LPC) and Common Professional Exam (CPE) where applicable.

Further information
More details can be found on our website.

WWW.CHOICESONLINE.COM

Pinsent Curtis . . . . www.pinsent.com
Reynolds Porter Chamberlain . . . . www.rpc.co.uk
Richards Butler . . . . www.richardsbutler.com

Richards Butler

RICHARDS BUTLER
INTERNATIONAL LAW FIRM

www.richardsbutler.com

gradrecruit@richardsbutler.com

15 St. Botolph Street, London, EC3A 7EE
t: 020 7772 5837

Business description:
Richards Butler is a premier international law firm with its head office in the City of London and lawyers based in a further 10 countries.

Graduates
We take 20 trainees each year. All applicants should have three B's at A-level or the equivilant and a 2:1 degree.

Training
Trainees spend 4 x 6 months seats and the option to take 2 x 3 months seats in various departments gaining broad experience of the firm. This can include a secondment to one of our overseas offices or clients. We will also pay all fees for your LPC and CPE.

Vacation schemes
We run 2 week vacation schemes in the summer for around 45 students. The scheme is open to both law and non-law students in at least their second year.

Apply
Applications for both the training contracts and vacation schemes should be made on-line. Go to www.richardsbutler.com

Rowe & Maw

www.roweandmaw.co.uk
roweandmaw@roweandmaw.com

11 Pilgrim Street, London, EC4V 6RW
t: 020 7248 4282 **f:** 020 7782 8790

Rowe and Maw is one of the UK's leading commercial law firms with 80 partners and offices in London, Manchester and Brussels.

S.J.Berwin & Co

www.sjberwin.com
graduate.recruitment@sjberwin.com

222 Grays Inn Road, London, WC1X 8HB
t: 020 7533 2268 **f:** 020 7533 2000

A leading city law firm with offices in London, Brussels, Madrid and Frankfurt and Munich.

Specialists in corporate finance, property, tax, employment, litigation and commercial law.

Opportunities:
Open days in Autumn and Spring Terms and a Summer Vacation Scheme runs annually.

Shoosmiths

Lawyers > Patent Lawyers

AA Thornton and company . . . . www.aathornton.co.uk
Abel & Imray. 020 7405 0203
David Keltie Associates . . . . www.keltie.com
Elkington and Fife . . . . www.elkfife.com
Forrester Ketley and Company. . . . . www.forresterketly.co.uk

Abel & Imray

020 7405 0203

20 Red Lion Street, London, WC1R 4PQ
t: 020 7405 0203

London (Head Office), Bath, Cardiff, Munich. Abel & Imray are a firm of Patent Attorneys and Trade Mark Attorneys

WWW.CHOICESONLINE.COM

Frank B Dehn and Company . . . . www.frankbdehn.co.uk

Marks & Clerk

www.marks-clerk.com

WWW.CHOICESONLINE.COM

Haseltine Lake . . . . www.haseltinelake.com
Hepworth Lawrence Bryer and Bizley . . . . www.hlbb.co.uk
J.A.Kemp and Company . . . . www.jakemp.co.uk
Kilburn and Strode. . . . . www.kstrode.co.uk
Marks & Clerk . . . . www.marks-clerk.com
Mathys and Squire . . . . www.mathys-squire.co.uk
Mewburn Ellis. . . . . www.mewburnellis.co.uk
Murgitroyd and Company. . . . . www.murgitroyd.co.uk
Page, White and Farrer. . . . . www.pagewhite.co.uk
Potts, Kerr and Co. www.pottskerr.co.uk
WP Thompson and Co.. . . . . www.wpthompson.co.uk

Management & Personnel

BOC . . . . www.bocgrads.co.uk
Chartered Institute of Personnel and Development (CIPD) . . . . .
. . . . www.cipd.co.uk
Cleanaway Limited . . . . www.cleanaway.co.uk

BOC

Chartered Institute of Personnel and Development (CIPD)

www.cipd.co.uk

CIPD House, Camp Road, London, SW19 4UX
t: 020 8971 9000 **f:** 020 8263 3333

The Chartered Institute of Personnel and Development (CIPD) is Europe's largest professional institute for all those concerned with people management and development.

The CIPD has 110,000 members and sets standards for professionals in the field. Grades of membership are determined by qualifications and attained experience, membership is highly respected and widely accepted by employers as requirements of practice.

Cleanaway Limited

Management Consultants

Bain & Company

www.bain.com

CHP Consulting

www.chp.co.uk
jog@chp.co.uk

6a Austin Friars, London, EC2N 2HA
t: 020 7588 1800

Accenture . . . . www.ac.com

Faithful & Gould

Faithful & **Gould**

www.fgould.com

77 Portland Place, London,
t: 020 7637 2345 **f:** 020 7580 8235

Faithful & Gould is one of the world's largest project and cost management consultancies with over 1400 staff and offices throughout the UK, Europe, USA and the Asia Pacific region.

Faithful & Gould Ltd is a member of the WS Atkins group of companies, committed to equal opportunities and fully accredited with Investors in People.

Deloitte Consulting

Deloitte & Touche

www.dc.com
ukgraduaterecruit@dc.com

Stoncutter Court, 1 Stonecutter Street, London, EC4A 4TR
t: 0800 323333 **f:** 020 7303 8177

N of vacancies: At least 100 high-calibre graduates to join analyst programme, focusing on strategy, process or technical aspects of major organisational change.

Disciplines involved: 2:1 hons degree in any subject and minimum of 24 UCAS points (excluding general studies) with some indication that you're highly numerate. You should also have a proven interest in business and the application of technology as an enabler of change within business

Locations: Full mobility is required. Offices located in 75 countries. UK offices located in London and Bath. All graduates will be offered London based contracts.

Application procedure: Please send your CV (including A-Level/Leaving Certificate grades) and a covering letter to Irene Oldham at the above address.

Deloitte Consulting is one of the world's leading e-Business consulting firms with over 11,500 consultants in more than 75 countries. The firm provides services to transform an entire enterprise - it's strategy, processes, information technology, and people.

WWW.CHOICESONLINE.COM

Bain and Company inc. UK . . . . www.bain.co.uk
Cap Gemini Ernst & Young. . . . . www.uk.cgey.co.uk
CHP Consulting . . . . www.chp.co.uk
Deloitte Consulting . . . . www.dc.com
Faithful & Gould . . . . www.fgould.com
Institute of Management Consultants . . . . www.imc.co.uk
McKinsey & Company . . . . www.mckinseyandcompany.co.uk
Metapraxis Ltd . . . . www.metaprixis.com
OpenLink Software . . . . www.openlink.co.uk
PA Consulting Group . . . . www.paconsulting.com
Perot Systems Corporation . . . . www.perotsystems.com
Saffery Champness . . . . www.saffery.com
Spectrum Strategy Consultants. . . . . . . www.spectrumstrategy.com
Towers Perrin/Tillinghast . . . . www.towers.com
Watson Wyatt Worldwide. . . . . www.watsonwyatt.com/graduate

Manufacturing Management

Alcatel Business Systems. . . . . www.alcatel.co.uk
British Aerospace plc . . . . www.baesystems.com/graduate
British American Tobacco . . . . www.bat.com
British Sugar. . . . . www.britishsugar.co.uk
Caradon plc . . . . www.caradon.com
CarnaudMetalbox . . . . www.crowncork.com
Celestica . . . . www.celestica.com
Chloride Group PLC . . . . www.chloridegroup.com
Corus Group . . . . www.corusgroup.com
DaimlerChrysler (UK) Ltd . . . . www.daimlerchrysler.co.uk
Dow Corning Ltd . . . . www.dowcorning.com

Milliken Industrials Limited

www.milliken.com

Celestica

www.celestica.com

Westfield House, West Avevue, Kidsgrove, Stoke-on-Trent,
Staffordshire, ST7 1TL
t: 01782 771000 **f:** 01782 785304

Disciplines involved: Minimum 2:2 in a relevant discipline.

Types of work offered: Engineering, operations management,
materials management, finance, human resources and
training.

Application procedure: Brochure and graduate application form
details available from Graduate Recruitment at the above
address

With more than 29,000 employees worldwide, Celestica operates
34 manufacturing and design facilities in the United States,
Canada, Mexico, the United Kingdom, Ireland, Italy, the Czech
Republic, Thailand, Hong Kong, China, Malaysia and Brazil.
Celestica provides a broad range of services including design,
prototyping, assembling, testing, product assurance, supply chain
management, worldwide distribution and after-sales service. Its
customers include industry leading original equipment
manufacturers (OEMs), primarily in the information technology
and communications sectors.

Ford Motor Company Ltd

www.ford.co.uk/recruitment

Rolls-Royce plc

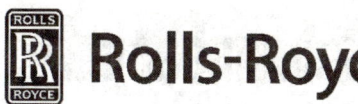

www.rolls-royce.com

65 Buckingham Gate, London, SW1E 6AT
t: 020 7222 9020

Disciplines involved: Any discipline.

N of vacancies: We have over 200 vacancies for graduate trainees each year. Industrial and vacation placements are also available.

Types of work offered: A wide range of engineering, commercial, procurement, finance, human resources, marketing and logistics opportunities.

Rolls-Royce plc is a global company providing power on land, sea and air. The company has established leading positions in civil aerospace, defence, marine and energy markets

Derby, Bristol, Glasgow

WWW.CHOICESONLINE.COM

ICI Group Recruitment. . . . . www.icigraduates.com
Jaguar Cars Ltd . . . . www.careers.jaguar.com
Milliken Industrials Limited . . . . www.milliken.com
Peugeot Motor Company plc . . . . www.peugeotcareers.co.uk
Philips Electronics UK Ltd . . . . www.phillips.co.uk
Pilkington. . . . . www.pilkington.com
Racal plc. . . . . www.racal-recruit.co.uk

Smiths Group

www.smiths-group.com

WWW.CHOICESONLINE.COM

Market Research

Ipsos UK Ltd www.research4um.co.uk

Ipsos UK Ltd

www.research4um.co.uk

King's House, Kymberley Road, Harrow, HA1 1PT
t: 020 8861 8000

No of vacancies: 12 Graduate Vacancies

Disciplines involved: A good degree in any subject, though some functions may require specific degree disciplines.

Careers offered: Research Executive, Computing and Statistics Executives.

Training & development: Both internal and external programmes, ensure graduates progress and develop in a dynamic and forward thinking business.

How to apply: For further information or to apply, please visit our website.

Media > Book Publishers

BMG Entertainment . . . . www.backstage-bmg.co.uk

Euromoney Institutional Investor PLC

www.euromoneyplc.com

Financial Times Group

www.ft.com

Macmillan Publishing

www.macmillan.co.uk

Houndmills, Basingstoke, Hampshire, RG21 6XS
t: 01256 329 242

Penguin UK

www.penguin.co.uk

27 Wrights Lane, London, W8 5TZ
t: 020 7416 3000

Butterworths . . . . www.butterworths.com
Euromoney Institutional Investor PLC . . www.euromoneyplc.com
Financial Times Group . . . . www.ft.com
Macmillan Publishing . . . . www.macmillan.co.uk
Penguin UK . . . . www.penguin.co.uk

Media > Film & Television

ARTTS International . . . . www.artts.co.uk
BBC . . . . www.bbc.co.uk/info/working
BMG Entertainment . . . . www.backstage-bmg.co.uk
Burson-Marsteller . . . . www.bm.com
Pearson Plc . . . . www.pearson.com

The Graduate Recruitment Company

www.graduate-recruitment.co.uk

Alhambra House, 27-31 Charing Cross Road,
London, WC2H 0AU
t: 020 7565 3429

With more Media vacancies than any other graduate recruitment agency in the UK we are The Graduate Recruitment Agency to deal with. More Jobs, more Employers, more choices.

Media > Magazine Publishers

IPC Magazines

www.ipc.co.uk

Kings Reach Tower, Stamford Street, London, SE1 9LS
t: 020 7261 5000

Conde Nast UK

www.condenast.co.uk

Vogue House, Hanover Square, London, W1S 1JU

VNU Business Publications

www.vnu.co.uk

32 - 34 Broadwick Street, London, W1A 2HG
t: 020 7316 9000 **f:** 0207 316 9020

Business Description:
VNU is one of the world's leading media and information companies employing thousands of people worldwide. We have leading positions in marketing information, business information, dirextories, consumer information and educational information.

No. of Vacancies:
A list of current vacancies and job descriptions is available on our web-site at www.vnu.com

Medical & Healthcare

British Pharmacological Society . . . . www.bps.ac.uk

Institute of Physics and Engineering in Medicine

www.ipem.org.uk

Fairmount House, 230 Tadcaster House, York, YO24 1ES

British United Provident Association (BUPA)

www.bupa.co.uk

BUPA is a global health and care organisation employing over 40,000 employees worldwide.

Graduates are recruited into Group General Management Programmes, which include the option to specialise in HR, Marketing and Finance or alternatively a Specialist IS Programme.

For further information and details of how to apply please see the website.

NHS Management Training Scheme

www.nhs.uk/futureleaders

Nurserve

www.nurserve.co.uk

Oils & Chemicals

BP Plc

www.bpfutures.com/uk

The Recruitment Team, Freepost 3310, Glasgow, G2 5XJ
t: 0800 027 7400 **f:** 0141 270 1234

No of vacancies: We have 75-100 vacancies for graduates in the UK.

Opportunities available: For those with specialist technical degrees, we have opportunities in engineering, (mechanical, electrical, petroleum/reservoir, drilling, chemical), chemistry + geoscience.

We also have a commercial early development programme that includes opportunities in sales, marketing, trading, logistics, HR and procurement/supply chain management for graduates of all disciplines.

We require a minimum of an upper 2nd Class Honours degree.

Application procedure: We have an on-line application form, which you can access via www.bpfutures.com/uk

More company information and our recruitment selection process details are available on-line at www.bpfutures.com/uk

If you are unable to access a computer you can get application forms from your careers advisory service or call our student helpline 0800 027 7400.

Croda

www.croda.com/careers

Cowick Hall, Snaith, Goole, East Yorkshire, DN14 9AA

Croda are a multinational supplier of natural plant extracts to the food, cosmetics and manufacturing industries.

ExxonMobil

www.exxonmobil.com/ukrecruitment

Freepost 17 LON 17093, London, W1E 4AZ
t: 0845 120 0292

BASF . . . . www.basf-plc.co.uk
BP Plc . . . . www.bpfutures.com/uk
Croda . . . . www.croda.com/careers
Enterprise Oil plc . . . . www.entoil.com

Science Recruitment Group

www.srg.co.uk

Buckland House, Langley Business Park, Slough, Berks, SL3 6EZ
t: 01753 589700

For contract, permanent and senior management positions within science based industries.

Kvaerner Oil & Gas Ltd (Maintenance, Modifications and Operations)

KVÆRNER™

www.kvaerner.com

Howe Moss Avenue, Kirkhill Industrial Estate, Dyce,
Aberdeen, AB21 0GP
t: 01224 414 515 **f:** 01224 414498

Business description: Kvaerner is a world-class Anglo-Norwegian supplier to the oil/gas industry with the capability and resources to undertake the world's most challenging projects.

N of vacancies: There are 4-6 vacancies.

Disciplines: Knowledge of engineering, commercial and IT is required due to the nature of the company.

Application procedure: Apply in writing enclosing a full up-to-date CV.

Opportunities available: Training is given as required for the job positions. Initial professional development programme is available, leading to chartered membership of professional institutions.

Kvaerner requires people with the willingness to learn new skills and to work as a team as well as on their own initiative.

WWW.CHOICESONLINE.COM

ExxonMobil . . . . www.exxonmobil.com/ukrecruitment

Ove Arup

www.arup.com

Chancery House, 53-64 Chancery Lane, London, WC2A 1QS

WWW.CHOICESONLINE.COM

TotalFinaElf Exploration UK PLC

TOTAL FINA ELF

www.totalfinaelf.com

Crawpeel Road, Altens, Aberdeen, AB12 3FG

t: 01224 297000 **f:** 01224 296972

Business description: TotalFinaElf Exploration UK PLC, one of the major oil and gas operators in the North Sea, employs around 630 staff and is headquartered in Aberdeen. It is a subsidiary of the international TotalFinaElf Group.

Opportunities available: We offer many opportunities for jobs and careers in the fields of R & D, chemical & process engineering, geoscience, production & maintenance operations and finance.

Application procedure: Please write to Karen Hutchinson, Snr H.R. Advisor Training & Development e-mail karen.hutchinson@tfeeuk.co.uk

U O P Ltd

www.uop.com

Liongate, Ladymead, Guildford, Surrey, GU1 1AT

t: 01483 304 848

UOP is a leader in developing and commercializing technology for license to the oil refining, petrochemical and gas processing industries. It is the largest process licensing organisation in the world.

Contact us online for more information.

Shell

www.shell.com
www.shell.com/careers
Response@si.shell.com

Rowlandsway House, Rowlandsway, Manchester, M22 5SB
t: 0845 600 1819 **f:** 0161 499 4859

N of vacancies: We have approximately 500 graduate vacancies worldwide.

Disciplines involved: Any discipline will be considered although for Technical vacancies a relevant degree subject is required.

Type of work offered: Engineering, Finance, Marketing and Sales, Supply Chain, Information Technology, eBusiness, Human Resources, Trading and Research.

Locations: Over 120 countries worldwide.

Application procedure: For an application form visit our website or telephone 0845 600 1819.

Shell is at the heart of the energy and petrochemical business, and one of the world's most successful organisations. Our business is unique. It not only has a huge impact on global development, but also offers international career prospects and outstanding challenges.

WWW.CHOICESONLINE.COM

PGS Exploration (UK) Ltd

www.pgs.com

Shell . . . . www.shell.com
TotalFinaElf Exploration UK PLC . . . . www.totalfinaelf.com
U O P Ltd . . . . www.uop.com

Pharmaceuticals

Amgen

www.amgen.com

Amgen . . . . www.amgen.com
AstraZeneca PLC . . . . www.ideas.astrazeneca.com
Biotechnology and Biological Sciences Research Council . . . .
. . . . www.bbsrc.ac.uk
Boots Contract Manufacturing . . . . www.bootscareers.com
Brewer Morris www.a1plc.co.uk
GlaxoSmithKline . . . . www.sb.com

Pfizer Ltd

www.pfizer.co.uk/recruit
www.workwithpfizer.co.uk

Ramsgate Road, Sandwich, Kent, CT13 9NJ
t: 01304 616 161

Sandwich (Head Office), London, New York Pfizer Ltd, is an international pharmaceutical company

AstraZeneca PLC

www.ideas.astrazeneca.com

15 Stanhope Gate, London, W1K 1LN
t: 0800 073 0403

No of vacancies: 100

Disciplines involved: Varies depending on which function graduates are recruited to

Recruited to: Chemistry (discovery, process, analytical) Biological Sciences, Pharmacy, Process Engineering, Engineering, Operations, Information Services, Human Resources, Sales and Marketing, Statistics

Location: AstraZeneca's main UK locations are in the South East, South West, North West and the Midlands.

Application procedure: Visit our website for further information or call 0800 0730403 for a brochure.

We are one of the largest pharmaceutical companies with a powerful range of products which address serious health problems. Our business is strategically focused on seven major therapeutic areas including cancer, heart disease and gastrointestinal disorders.

Merck Sharp & Dohme (Holdings) Ltd

www.merck.com
www.msd-uk.co.uk

Property

AYH plc

www.ayh.com

40 Clifton Street, London, EC2A 4AY
t: 020 7377 6666

London (Head Office), Birmingham, Manchester, Leeds, Edinburgh

AYH plc are property and construction consultants providing project management, cost consultancy and quantity surveying, facilities consultancy, building surveying, engineering services consultancy and CDM compliance services to clients in the UK and overseas.

GVA Grimley

www.gvagrimley.co.uk
mce@gvagrimley.co.uk

Group Personnel Office, 3 Brindley Place, Birmingham, B1 2JB
t: 0870 900 8990

GVA Grimley is a partnership of International Property Advisors with offices in London West End and City, Birmingham, Bristol, Cardiff, Manchester, Leeds, Edinburgh, Glasgow, Belgium and Australia.

Weatherall Green & Smith

www.weatheralls.co.uk

22 Chancery Lane, London, WC2A 1LT

Weatherall Green & Smith forms part of one of the largest real estate consultancies in Europe, delivering strategic solutions to occupiers and investors. We recruit 10-20 graduates every year. The majority enter our General Practice Division but we also take a limited number of Building Surveying and Planning & Development graduates.

Public Relations

August.One Communications

AUGUST.ONE
COMMUNICATIONS

www.augustone.com

Network House, Wood Lane, London, W12 7SL
t: 020 8434 5555

Chime Communications

www.chime-plc.co.uk

14 Curzon Street, London, W1J 5HN

Every Autumn we recruit seven graduates on a 12 month fixed contract. During this year our graduates spend three months with four of our Group companies.

The advantage of our programme is that graduates experience four different communications disciplines first hand, working in four very different companies each with their own culture.

If you are interested in applying please visit our website.

Bell Pottinger Communications . . . . www.bell-pottinger.co.uk
Biss Lancaster Euro RSCG . . . . www.bisslancaster.com

Countrywide Porter Novelli

www.countrywidepn.co.uk

31 St Petersburgh Place, London, WC2 4LA

We are the UK's fifth largest Public Relations consultancy. As a full service consultancy, our work ranges from communications strategy development and crisis management to product launches and brand building. We have specialist consultants in areas such as financial services, healthcare and technology as well as expertise in consumer and business communications.

Grayling Group

Grayling Group

www.graylinggroup.com

4 Bedford Square, London, WC1B 3RA
t: 020 7255 1100 **f:** 020 7631 0602

The Grayling Group is an International Network of Public Relations and Public Affairs companies whose activities extend beyond the UK and Europe to the United States and Pacific Rim.

Brodeur Worldwide	www.brodeur.com
BSMG Worldwide (UK)	www.bsmg.com
Buchanan Communications	www.buchanan.uk.com
Burson-Marsteller	www.bm.com
Chime Communications	www.chime-plc.co.uk
Citigate Dewe Rogerson	www.incepta.com
Cohn & Wolfe	www.cohnwolfe.com
College Hill	www.collegehill.com
Countrywide Porter Novelli	www.countrywidepn.co.uk
Edelman Public Relations Worldwide	www.edelman.com
Financial Dynamics	www.fd.com
Firefly Communications	www.fireflycomms.com
Fishburn Hedges	www.fishburnhedges.com

Institute of Public Relations

www.ipr.org.uk

The Old Trading House, 15 Northburgh Street, London, EC1V OPR
t: 020 7253 5151 ext 238

Ketchum

www.ketchumcomms.co.uk
hr@ketchumcomms.co.uk

35 - 41 Folgate Street, London, E1 6BX
t: 020 7611 3500

Career Opportunities at Ketchum
Ketchum prides itself on being a people business and we are committed to recruiting, developing and keeping the brightest and best in the business.

Ketchum CareerTrack
Ketchum is a continuous learning organisation. Everyone at every level of the company has a Personal Development Plan and receives regular 360 appraisals and training to help them develop their professional and management skills.

Ketchum London is an exciting place to work
Based in the center of the Capital, the London team works and plays hard. Over the past three years, the office has grown from 24 to 155 staff and from a handful to 70 major clients, making it the fastest growing of the large agencies in the UK.

Fleishman-Hillard U.K. Ltd. . . . . www.fleishman.com
Freud Communications . . . . www.freudcommunications.com
Golin/Harris International . . . . www.golinharris.com
Good Relations . . . . www.goodrelations.co.uk
Grayling Group . . . . www.graylinggroup.com
Harrison Cowley . . . . www.harrisoncowley.com
Hill & Knowlton (UK) . . . . www.hillandknowlton.com
Institute of Public Relations . . . . www.ipr.org.uk
Ketchum . . . . www.ketchumcomms.co.uk
Medical Action Communications Ltd . . . . . . www.medicalaction.com

Public Sector

Benefits Agency . . . . www.dss.gov.uk/ba

Department for Education and Skills

department for
education and skills
creating opportunity, releasing potential, achieving excellence

www.dfee.gov.uk

Coxton House, 6-12 Tothill Street, London, SW19 9NF
t: 020 7273 3000

The Department of Education and Skills is a UK Government department. Our aim is to give everyone the opportunity to fulfill their potential through education, training and work.

We have vacancies for administrators, managers, research assistants, senior managers and public appointments.

Details of all our vacancies can be found on the website above.

Government Statistical Service

www.statistics.gov.uk/gssjobs

Office for National Statistics, GSS Personnel, Zone D4/22, 1 Drummond Gate, London, SW1V 2QQ
t: 020 7533 5040 **f:** 020 7533 5044

Minimum required: 2:2 Numerate Degree

Types of work offered: Temporary and permanent

Departments in London, Bath, Bootle, Cardiff, Darlington, Edinburgh, Glasgow, Leeds, Newcastle, Newport, Portsmouth, Sheffield, Southend, Titchfield and York.

Civil Service Fast Stream

www.faststream.gov.uk

Innovation Court, New Street, Basingstoke, Hampshire,
RG21 7JB
t: 01256 383610

Child Support Agency . . . . www.dss.gov.uk/csa

Forestry Commission

Forestry Commission

www.forestry.gsi.gov.uk

231 Corstorphine Road, Edinburgh, EH12 7AT
t: 0131 334 0303 **f:** 0131 314 6174

Business description: The Forestry Commission is the Government Department responsible for forestry throughout Great Britain. We have a mission to continue protecting Britain's forests and woodlands and increase their value to society and the environment.

N of vacancies: We have approximately 60 vacancies in various disciplines each year.

Opportunities available: We provide training for our employees to the standards needed for their job placement and the company needs.

Application procedure: Positions are advertised in national/local press and application forms can be obtained by telephoning the contact point shown in the advertisement.

More information is available on our web-site at: www.forestry.gsi.gov.uk

Government Legal Service

recruit@gls.gsi.gov.uk

GLS Recruitment Team, Queen Anne's Chambers, 28 Broadway, SW1H 9JS

t: 020 7210 3304

The Government Legal Service consists of around 1500 qualified lawyers (solicitors and barristers) employed in about 40 government organisations.

The GLS also has a small number of opportunities for summer placements, training contracts and pupillages.

Enquiries should be directed to the GLS Recruitment Team above.

HM Treasury

www.hm-treasury.gov.uk

Allington Towers, 19 Allington street, London, SW1E 5EB

t: 020 7270 1338 **f:** 020 7270 1353

Vacancies

A list of current vacancies is available on our web-site at www.hm-treasury.gov.uk and is updated daily.

Opportunities

We are committed to developing you, so we offer every opportunity for you to acquire the necessary skills and knowledge you need to do your job well - and prepare for more challenging work if you want it. The training period is two years and our experts provide tailored training and devlopment needs.

Application

Application forms are available on-line along with recruitment brochures. If you have any further questions or general queries about our graduate scheme, please contact Louise Woolard on 020 7270 1356 or write to the above address.

More information the company or our recruitment scheme is available on our web-site at www.hm-treasury.gov.uk

HM Prison Service Graduate Accelerated Promotion Scheme to Prison Governor Grade

www.hmprisonservice.gov.uk

MSSU, Room 329 HM Prison Service, Cleland House, Page Street, London   SW1P 4LN
t: 020 7217 6437 **f:** 020 7217 2951

Salary: Salary starts at ú15,842 and rises in two stages, after promotion, to circa ú30,000.

Application procedure: Please apply to Miles Layton at the above address. Our recruitment process is an annual process and normally commences in September and concludes in April.

Experience: The opportunity to develop your management potential and equip you with high-quality personal and technical skills. The scheme also affords the opportunity to work in a wide variety of prisons.

Opportunities available: Opportunities are always available to progress and better your level of job satisfaction.

Disciplines: You should have or expect to gain an honours degree or equivalent qualification in any subject discipline. Experience or interest in personnel or institutional management, law, penology, psychology or social studies is helpful, but not essential.

The Patent Office

www.patent.gov.uk
enquiries@patent.gov.uk

Inland Revenue

www.inlandrevenue.gov.uk

3rd Floor, Mowbray House, PO Box 55, Castle Meadow Rd, Nottingham, NG2 1BE
t: 0115 974 0596 **f:** 0115 974 0611

Graduate telephone & email: 0115 974 0606 recruitment.ir@gnet.gov.uk

Opportunities available: There are two graduate recruitment schemes: the Inspector Training Programme and the Fast Stream Development Programme.

N of vacancies: Up to 95 over both schemes.

Degree required: A first or second class honours degree in any discipline.

Other requirements: Applicants must be UK nationals.

When to apply: May/June of each year with a view to start in the following February for the Inspector Training Programme. Oct-Nov of each year for a start in July the following year for Fast Stream.

The Inland Revenue aims to provide an effective and fair tax service to the country and Government.

WWW.CHOICESONLINE.COM

NHS Management Training Scheme

www.nhs.uk/futureleaders
mtsinfo@mts.nhs.uk

NHS Leadership Centre, Management Training Schemes, 40 Eastbourne Terrace, London, W2 3QR
t: 01325 745 818

Business Description:
The NHS is the largest employer in Europe. With 1 million staff and a ú48bn budget, it's the ideal training ground for a career at the leading edge of public sector management.

No of Vacancies:
We have approximately 60 vacancies each year for general management and 70 vacancies for financial management.

Training:
The general management training scheme offers a two-year programme of training and development combining early responsibility in work placements with a challenging educational programme. The financial management training scheme is a 40 month programme that combines an accountancy qualification with management development.

Benefits:
We offer a starting salary of around ú17,500 (excluding London allowance), rising in the second and third years of training.

More company and recruitment information is available on our web-site at www.nhs.uk/futureleaders

WWW.CHOICESONLINE.COM

Metropolitan Police Service . . . . www.met.police.uk
MI5. . . . . www.mi5.gov.uk
Ministry of Agriculture, Fisheries & Food . . . . www.maff.gov.uk
Ministry of Defense . . . . www.mod.uk

National Insurance Contributions Office ....
.... www.inlandrevenue.gov.uk
NHS Management Training Scheme ... www.nhs.uk/futureleaders
Security Service, The (MI5) www.mi5.gov.uk
The Patent Office .... www.patent.gov.uk

Public Sector > Police Authorities

Avon & Somerset Police Authority ....
.... www.avonandsomerset.police.uk
Bedfordshire Police Authority ....
.... www.bedfordshirepoliceauthority.co.uk
Cambridgeshire Police Authority .... www.cambs.police.uk
Cheshire Police Authority .... www.cheshire.police.uk
City Of London Police Authority .... www.cityoflondon.gov.uk
Dyfed-Powys Police Authority .... www.dyfed-powys.police.uk
Essex Police Authority .... www.essex.police.uk
Gloucestershire Police Authority .... www.glouscc.gov.uk
Greater Manchester Police Authority .... www.gmpa.gov.uk
Gwent Police Authority .... www.gwent.police.uk
Hampshire Police Authority .... www.hampshire.police.uk
Humberside Police Authority .... www.humberside-pa.org.uk
Kent Police Authority .... www.kent.police.uk
Lancashire Police Authority .... www.lancashire.police.uk

Merseyside Police Authority

www.merseyside.police.uk

West House, Mercury Court,
Tithebarn Street, Liverpool, L69 2NU

Leicestershire Police Authority . . . . www.leics.police.uk
Lincolnshire Police Authority . . . . www.lincs.police.uk
Merseyside Police Authority . . . . www.merseyside.police.uk
Metropolitan Police Authority . . . . www.mpa.gov.uk
North Yorkshire Police Authority . . . . www.nypa.org.uk
Northamptonshire Police Authority . . . . www.northants.police.uk
Northern Ireland Police Authority . . . . www.pani.org.uk
Northumbria Police Authority . . . . www.northumbria.police.uk
Nottinghamshire Police Authority. . . . .
. . . . www.nottinghamshire.police.uk
South Wales Police Authority . . . . www.south-wales.police.uk
South Yorkshire Police Authority . . . . www.southyorks.org.uk
Staffordshire Police Authority . . . . www.staffordshire.gov.uk
Suffolk Police Authority . . . . www.suffolk.police.uk
Surrey Police Authority . . . . www.surreypa.gov.uk
Sussex Police Authority . . . . www.sussex.police.uk

West Midlands Police Authority

www.west-midlands.police.uk

Lloyd House, Colmore Circus,
Birmingham, B4 6NQ

If you're considering a career in the police service or are just curious about what it can offer, you'll find all the answers here.

We are one of the UK's largest and most progressive police services. Step inside and share our vision.

Suffolk Police Authority

www.suffolk.police.uk

St. Helen Court, County Hall, Ipswich, IP4 2JS

West Mercia Police Authority . . . . www.westmercia.police.uk
West Midlands Police Authority . . . www.west-midlands.police.uk
Wiltshire Police Authority . . . . www.wiltshire.police.uk

Recruitment

Aerotek Europe www.recruit4aerotek.co.uk
Calibre Recruitment . . . . www.calibre-recruitment.co.uk
Graduate Recruitment Bureau . . . . www.grb.uk.com

Aerotek Europe

www.recruit4aerotek.co.uk

230 Wharfedale Road, Winnersh Triangle, Wokingham,
Berkshire, RG41 5TP
t: 0118 377 9900 **f:** 0118 377 9729

No of vacancies: Approximately 150

Disciplines involved: Any discipline - 2:1 minimum

Work offered: Recruitment Sales, Finance, Customer Service.

Locations: Reading, London, Hitchin, Coventry, Manchester,
Edinburgh, High Wycombe, Windsor, Holland, Germany.

Application procedure: Company application form or online
from the company website.

Aerotek Europe is a Multinational Technical Recruitment
Consultancy. We are a market leader operating within the IT,
telecommunications, engineering and administrative sectors.

Calibre Recruitment

www.calibre-recruitment.co.uk
careers@calibre-recruitment.co.uk

Unit 10 River Court, Riverside Park, Middlesbrough, TS2 1RT
t: 01642 244020 **f:** 01642 243480

Contact: Elaine Crosby

Number of consultants: 3 (perm)

Specialisations: Graduate recruitment across all disciplines including Engineering, IT, Sales and Marketing, Scientific, HR etc.

Salary range: ú12,000 - ú50,000

Geography covered: North East

Manpower . . . . www.manpower.co.uk

Graduate Recruitment Bureau

www.grb.uk.com
info@grb.uk.com

Cornelius House, 178-182 Church Road, Hove, East Sussex, BN3 2DJ
t: 01273 325775 **f:** 01273 325003

The Graduate Recruitment Bureau is a leading employment agency for finalists and graduates run by graduates. We target a number of companies for you and define a precise job specification based on the role, career progression, salary, benefits, travel, promotion prospects and future development.

Science Recruitment Group

www.srg.co.uk

Buckland House, Langley Business Park, Slough, Berks,
SL3 6EZ
t: 01753 589700

For contract, permanent and senior management positions within
science based industries.

The Graduate Recruitment Company

www.graduate-recruitment.co.uk

Alhambra House, 27-31 Charing Cross Road, London,
WC2H 0AU
t: 020 7565 3429

With more Recruitment vacancies than any other graduate
recruitment agency in the UK we are The Graduate Recruitment
Agency to deal with. More Jobs, more Employers, more choices.

Retail > Fashion

Arcadia Group plc

www.arcadiagroup.co.uk

Colegrave House, 70 Berners Street, London, W1P 3AE
t: 020 7291 2390

Monsoon & Accessorize Ltd

www.monsoon.co.uk

Monsoon is a design-led retailer that retails a wide range of women's clothing, children's wear, fragrance, and the Monsoon Home range.

Monsoon's objective is to provide it's customers with an experience that is distinctively different, in terms of both product offering and levels of customer service. Monsoon recognises that its people, and in particular its continuing ability to inspire, motivate and reward them, are critical to the achievement of this aim.

Arcadia Group plc	www.arcadiagroup.co.uk
Clarks International	www.clarks.com
Debenhams	www.debenhams.co.uk
Decathlon	www.decathlon.com

Vogue Magazine

www.vogue.co.uk

Are you looking for a job in fashion? We have opportunities for everyone from the hopeful, young design graduate to the experienced retail executive.

Next Retail Ltd

www.next.co.uk

Desford Road, Enderby, Leicester, LE9 5AT
t: 0116 286 6411 **f:** 0116 284 2359

Business description: Next is a fast and exciting business which employs 1,000's of staff and has an excellent customer relationship.

Opportunities available: Next want their employees to feel challenged and will reward them well and offer good training opportunities for personal development and career growth.

Application procedure: Apply in writing enclosing a full and up-to-date CV to the above address.

Disciplines: Next do not always insist on degree qualifications, as long as you show good potential in a relevent discipline, you will be considered.

For more information go on-line @ www.next.co.uk

Marks and Spencer Plc . . . . www.marks-and-spencer.com

Primark

www.primark.co.uk
hrrecruit@primark.co.uk

Primark House, 41 West Street, Reading, Berkshire, RG1 1TT

Primark is a major retail group employing over 8,000 people. Primark operates over 110 stores in the UK and Ireland, where it trades under the Penneys name.

Retail > Food

ALDI GmbH & Co

www.aldi.com

Sheepcotes, Springfield Business Park, Chelmsford,
CM2 5AS

Successful management of our people is central to our business philosophy. We place high expectations on those we employ who we, in return, motivate and reward well above the average.

McDonalds Restaurants Ltd

www.mcdonalds.co.uk

Everyone knows McDonald's - we're one of the world's top brands. We're a world leader in the food service business and we didn't get there by accident.

Our principles of quality, service and cleanliness start with our people. We train our top quality managers to drive the business through every restaurant in the UK.

And we're opening up to 100 new restaurants every year, creating managerial opportunities for dynamic leaders, just like you.

Asda Stores Ltd

www.asda.co.uk

ASDA House, Great Wilson Street, Leeds, West Yorks,
LS11 5AD
t: 0113 243 5435 **f:** 0113 241 7732

Business description: Asda, Britain's best value food and clothing
superstore, became part of the Wal-Mart family on 26 July 1999.
The company was formed in 1965 by a group of farmers from
Yorkshire, and now has 240 stores and 19 depots across the UK.

We employ 100,000 colleagues who have a reputation for being
the best and the friendliest in the industry, and we work with over
2,800 suppliers. Our stores are "stores of the community", playing
a positive part in all aspects of local life.

WWW.CHOICESONLINE.COM

Majestic Wine Warehouses Ltd

www.majestic.co.uk

We are currently opening 8-10 nw stores every year, and need to
recruit high-quality trainee managers of graduate calibre. If you're
interested, you may want to come and see us at one of the careers
fairs we'll be attending in October and November.

Students looking to spend time in a retail placement for their
'sandwich year' can also join Majestic on one-year placements. We
are also in need of Sales Assistants and drivers, particularly
within the M25.

WWW.CHOICESONLINE.COM

Oddbins

www.oddbins.com

31 - 33 Weir Road, London, SW19 8UG
t: 020 8944 4428

Marks and Spencer Plc . . . . www.marks-and-spencer.com

Sainsburys

www.sainsburys.co.uk/fresherthinking

Graduate Recruitment Department, Stamford House,
Stamford Street, London, SE1 9LL

Launch your career with Sainsbury's and discover challenging and rewarding opportunities in Retail, Buying, Marketing, Supply Chain, Finance, Human Resources, Quality & Innovation and Pharmacy.

McDonalds Restaurants Ltd . . . . www.mcdonalds.co.uk
Oddbins . . . . www.oddbins.com

Tesco Stores Ltd

www.tesco.com/graduates

Graduate Recruitment Department, Tesco Stores Ltd, Tesco House, PO Box 506, Cardiff, CF14 4TS
t: 0870 600 6067 **f:** 01992 647 290

Disciplines involved: Store management, Tesco.com, HR management, Finance, IT, site and strategic research.

Minimum required: 2:2 for stores, 2:1 for other schemes.

Tesco is a global business and the no.1 UK food retailer.

Punch Retail . . . . www.punch-retail.co.uk
Safeway Stores plc . . . . www.safeway.co.uk
Sainsburys . . . . www.sainsburys.co.uk
Tesco Stores Ltd . . . . www.tesco.com/recruitment

Retail > General

Boots Healthcare International . . . . www.bootscareers.com

Harrods Ltd

www.harrods.com

Training Schemes Department,
Harrods Ltd, Knightsbridge,
London, SW1X 7XL

WWW.CHOICESONLINE.COM

John Lewis Partnership

www.johnlewis.co.uk

WWW.CHOICESONLINE.COM

Do It All . . . . www.focusdoitall.co.uk
Halfords . . . . www.halfords.co.uk
Harrods Ltd . . . . www.harrods.com
John Lewis Partnership . . . . www.johnlewis.co.uk
Phones4U . . . . www.caudwell.com/grad

Phones4U

www.caudwell.com/grad

Milton Hollins, Shelton Old Road,
Stoke on Trent, ST4 7RY

WWW.CHOICESONLINE.COM

Unilever plc

Unilever

www.unilever.com

www.ucmds.com (on-line application)

unilever@barkers-response.co.uk (for brochure & application form)

PO Box 1538, Slough PDO, SL1 1YT
t: 0870 154 3550

N of vacancies: We have 18,000 employees in the UK and approximately 100 vacancies.

Disciplines involved: Any honours degree (except for Innovation and Technology Management, and Manufacturing and Supply chain, where specific degrees are required).

Types of work offered: Marketing, Customer Management (FMCG and Business to Business), Financial Management, Human Resources, Information Management, Innovation and Technology Management, and Manufacturing and Supply Chain.

Application procedure: Company brochure and online application form both available from the above sources.

Unilever is one of the worlds leading consumer goods companies, dedicated to meeting the everyday needs of people everywhere. Worldwide we employ a quarter of a million people with a turnover of ú27 billion.

WHSmith

www.whsmith.co.uk
www.whsmith-recruitment.co.uk
grads@group-whsmith.co.uk

Greenbridge Road, Swindon, Wiltshire, SN3 3LD
t: 01793 562433

WWW.CHOICESONLINE.COM

Sales

A F Selection Ltd . . . . www.afselection.co.uk
Arcadia Group plc . . . . www.arcadiagroup.co.uk/recruitment
AstraZeneca PLC. . . . . www.ideas.astrazeneca.com

BOC

www.bocgrads.co.uk

WWW.CHOICESONLINE.COM

Cauldwell Group

www.cauldwell.com

WWW.CHOICESONLINE.COM

BOC . . . . www.bocgrads.co.uk
Cadbury Schweppes . . . . www.cadburyschweppes.com
Cauldwell Group. . . . . www.cauldwell.com
Decathlon . . . . www.decathlon.com
ExxonMobil. . . . . www.exxonmobil.com/ukrecruitment
Friends Provident . . . . www.friendsprovident.co.uk
GlaxoSmithKline . . . . www.sb.com

Friends Provident

www.friendsprovident.co.uk

Mars

www.mars.com/university
mars.graduate@eu.effem.com

Graduate Marketing, Dundee Road, Slough, Berks, SL1 4JX
t: 017 5351 4999

Working at Mars is different. From day 1 we offer unrivalled stimulation, challenge and opportunity to high calibre graduates.

No. of vacancies: Mars Management Training Programme: 20-25 Other Programmes: 15-20

Disciplines involved: MMTP - Any disciplines

Opportunities available: MMTP - Sales, Marketing, Production Manufacturing, Research & Development, Engineering, commercial, logistics, finance, personnel. Functional Programmes - Finance, Engineering, Software Engineering, IT

Locations: Thames Valley, Leeds, Leicestershire.

Hotline: 017 5351 4999

Mars Incorporated is a world leader in each of its main businesses: branded snack foods, petcare products, main meal foods, automated payment systems and drinks vending. We are a truly international business with over 140 sites in more than 60 countries worldwide and have an annual turnover in excess of $13 billion.

Scientists

Amgen

www.amgen.com

Atomic Weapons Establishment plc

www.awe.co.uk

Amgen . . . . www.amgen.com
Atomic Weapons Establishment plc . . . . www.awe.co.uk
Biotechnology and Biological Sciences Research Council . . . .
. . . . www.bbsrc.ac.uk
Derwent Information Ltd . . . . www.derwent.co.uk
DESG . . . . www.desg.mod.uk

Biotechnology and Biological Sciences Research Council

www.bbsrc.ac.uk

Organon Laboratories Ltd

www.organon.com
persman@organon.nhe.akzonobel.nl

Newhouse, Lanarkshire, ML1 5SH
t: 01698 736000

Ortho Biotech

www.orthobiotech.co.uk

PO Box 79, Saunderton, High Wycombe, Buckinghamshire, HP14 4HJ

Parexel

www.parexel.com

Science Recruitment Group

www.srg.co.uk

Buckland House,
Langley Business Park,
Slough, Berks, SL3 6EZ
t: 01753 589700

For contract, permanent and senior management positions within science based industries.

QinetiQ

QinetiQ

www.QinetiQ.com/careers
grad-recruit@QinetiQ.com
Fraser, Eastney, Portsmouth, Hampshire, PO4 9LJ
t: 023 9233 5588 **f:** 020 9233 4579

Main Activities

QinetiQ is a world-leader in the creation and application of technology. As the newly privatised arm of the former DERA, this dynamic organisation has a store of expertise that is admired worldwide, and a culture inspired by free-thinking and ground-breaking research.

Opportunities

Each year we recruit 400 analytically minded, innovative graduates from most science, engineering, IT and numerate degrees. Graduates are recruited to a wide range of challenging and interesting careers, including roles in development work, operational analysis, scientific research, test & evaluation and project management.

Training

QinetiQ offers an individually designed programme of specialist and management training. MSc and PhD sponsorship, international exchange programmes and project management development.

Salaries

Up to ú21,000 dependent upon qualifications and experience. Salary progression is determined upon performance.

Locations

All QinetiQ locations lie outside main city areas. Our main sites are at Farnborough, Malvern, Portsmouth, Dorchester, Sevenoaks, Chertsey and Boscombe Down.

How to Apply

Apply on-line at www.QinetiQ.com/careers

Technology

Motorola Ltd

r57643@email.sps.mot.com
www.motorolacareers.com

Colvilles Road, Kelvin Industrial Estate, East Kilbride,
Glasgow, G75 0TG
t: 01355 355000

Business description: Motorola is a world leading provider of wireless communications, semiconductors and advanced electronic systems operating globally.

Opportunities available: We have a modular training programme which lasts for two years. We have unlimited opportunities for employees to develop there career further.

Application procedure: Application forms are available on-line or alternatively, you can e-mail us your CV along with a covering letter.

WWW.CHOICESONLINE.COM

Telecommunications

British Telecom . . . . www.bt.com/careers

British Telecom

www.bt.com/careers

BT is one of the world's leading providers of information and communications services and one of the largest private sector companies in Europe. Its key activities include local, long distance and international telecommunications services, mobile communications, internet services and IT solutions.

BT serves over 29 million fixed and 11 million mobile lines in the UK, as well as providing extensive network services to other licensed operators. Its presence worldwide includes mobile, internet and other operations and joint ventures in France, Spain, Sweden, Germany, New Zealand, Latin America and others.

Graduate Recruitment
Our graduate recruitment programme is open year round and offers opportunities in all areas of our business including IT, marketing, HR and technical sales

Training & deveopment
Graduate entrants benefit from BT's Graduate Development Programme which delivers excellent management development through a variety of training and development activities from Training Centre courses to Computer Based Training.

Opprtunities
Most BT people work in the UK but we do have limited opportunities to work abroad. BT supports 'work/life' balance and flexible working - where practical employees may have the option of working from home.

Motorola Ltd

r57643@email.sps.mot.com

www.motorolacareers.com

Colvilles Road, Kelvin Industrial Estate, East Kilbride, Glasgow, G75 0TG

t: 01355 355000 **f:** 01355 234582

Business description: Motorola is a world leading provider of wireless communications, semiconductors and advanced electronic systems operating globally.

Opportunities available: We have a modular training programme which lasts for two years. We have unlimited opportunities for employees to develop there career further.

Application procedure: Application forms are available on-line or alternatively, you can e-mail us your CV along with a covering letter.

Nokia

www.nokia.co.uk/careers

Cable & Wireless plc . . . . www.cwplc.com

Ericsson Ltd . . . . www.ericsson.com

One 2 One

www.one2one.co.uk

one2onework4@one2one.co.uk

Unisys

www.unisysukgrads.com

Vodafone plc

www.vodafone.co.uk/graduates

Types of work offered: Engineering, IT, Marketing, Finance and Human Resources.

Degrees required: You must have at least a 2.1. To join us as an Engineer, your degree must be in Engineering or a related subject; however, IT, HR, Finance and Marketing are open to graduates from more or varied disciplines.

N of vacancies: 50-100

Location: Predominantly Newbury.

Application procedure: For more information or to apply, please visit our website.

The world's leading mobile telecoms company
Vodafone set up the first analogue cellular network; introduced the first Global System for Mobile Communications (GSM); created the first prepaid service; was the first to offer text messaging and to trial WAP technology. Now we are developing wireless multimedia applications that will continue to revolutionise the way societies communicate.

A career with Vodafone will propel you to the forefront of one of the world's fastest growing industries.

Vodafone plc Continued

Where graduates fit in

Maintaining our success as one of the world's ten largest companies depends not only on recruiting the most talented people, but also on maintaining our unmatched commitment to first-class professional development. This allows everyone to maximise their potential, adding value to the services we provide.

We are looking for people with at least a 2.1 in any engineering subject to join us as engineers - and from any discipline to work in IT, Marketing, Finance or Human Resources. And it may surprise you to hear that you don't need a technical knowledge of telecoms. It's your aptitude for learning that interests us.

What's in it for you?

Superb training, mentoring, rapid career progression, generous rewards - it's all yours when you pursue a career with Vodafone.

You'll be working with people that are defining the industry's future as you progress through our structured, yet flexible development programme. Your personal mentor will help you navigate your way through a series of placements across the company, equipping you with a broad business overview and a wide range of specialist skills.

You'll get a competitive starting salary (Masters degrees, PhDs and relevant work experience will all increase this figure) followed by about four pay reviews in the first two years.

Secure your place at the forefront and visit us at www.vodafone.co.uk/graduates where you can apply online. The deadline is ongoing, although application before January is recommended.

Motorola Ltd	www.motorolacareers.com
Nokia	www.nokia.co.uk/careers
NTL	www.ntl.co.uk
One 2 One	www.one2one.co.uk
Unisys	www.unisysukgrads.com
Vodafone plc	www.vodafone.co.uk

Travel

Arriva plc . . . . www.arriva.co.uk
British Airways plc . . . . www.britishairwaysjobs.com

British Airways plc

www.britishairwaysjobs.com

WWW.CHOICESONLINE.COM

British Midland Airways . . . . www.flybmi.com
EasyJet . . . . www.easyjet.co.uk

Specialist Holidays Group

recruit@s-h-g.co.uk

overseasrecruitment@s-h-g.co.uk

King's Place, Wood Street, Kingston upon Thames, Surrey,
KT1 1SH
t: 0870 888 0028 **f:** 020 8541 2492

Business description:
SHG, the specialist division of the Thomson Travel Group
comprises 13 established tour operators including Crystal
Holidays, Thomson Ski, Simply Travel, Something Special and
Magic Travel Group. UK and overseas opportunities are available
throughout the group.

WWW.CHOICESONLINE.COM

Specialist Holidays Group . . . . www.shgjobs.co.uk
Virgin Airways . . . . www.virgin-atlantic.com

Utilities

ALSTOM UK Ltd. . . . . www.alstom.com

awg plc

www.anglianwater.co.uk

Anglian House, Ambury Road, Huntingdon, Cambridge,
PE18 6NZ
t: 01480 323 268 **f:** 01480 323 258

Business description: Anglian Water are part of the awg plc group of companies and one of the leading providers of water and wastewater services in the UK. Located in the east of England, we serve the needs of over 5 million industrial, commercial and domestic customers.

Opportunities available: We are recruiting a number of outstanding people on to our Graduate Development Programme which is designed to provide the opportunity to develop future business leaders within the group. Therefore applicants will need a good class of degree, along with first-class communication skills and the drive to succeed. There are opportunities in finance, engineering, business services IT and in our commercial companies.

Our graduate programme is structured to develop your professional, technical, managerial and personal skills through a series of placements and projects throughout our business, whilst also allowing you to control your own career focus.

More information can be found on-line at: www.anglianwater.co.uk

Baker Hughes INTEQ

www.bakerhughes.com
uk.recruitment@inteq.com

Barclayhill Place, Portlethen, Aberdeen, AB12 4PF
t: 01224 408000 **f:** 01224 408004

Business description: Baker Hughes is a leader in oilfield services. We create value for oil and gas producers by providing practical technology to find, produce and manage petroleum reservoirs.

N of vacancies: We have a number of vacancies for graduates in a variety of working environments.

Opportunities available: We have training programmes which are designed to improve existing skills and learn new ones.

Application procedure: Send an up-to-date CV along with a covering letter to the above address.

More information on Baker Hughes is available on-line at: www.bakerhughes.com

National Grid Company plc

www.nationalgrid.com
graduate.jobs@uk.ngrid.com

Kirby Corner Road, Coventry, CV4 8JY
t: 024 7653 7777 **f:** 024 7642 3678

Powergen UK plc

Westwood Way,
Westwood Business Park,
Coventry, CV4 8LG
t: 024 7642 4785
f: 024 7642 5045

www.powergenplc.com

Business description: We are the UK's leading integrated gas and electricity company, as well as provide telecom services and an internet provider.

Work offered: You will initially gain professional expertise within a specific work area although in the longer term you will acquire experience and in depth understanding across a variety of Powergen activities. We provide tailored training development programmes which are overseen by a mentor at management level.

N of vacancies: 20 approx.

Disciplines: We are particularly interested in engineering, IT & business related disciplines. We specify the minimum 2.1 honours degree or equivalent.

Salary: In addition to the first class training & development, we guarantee to provide every new graduate with a starting salary of circa ú19,000 plus benefits.

Application procedure: Details on how to apply are available on-line at: www.powergenplc.com/graduates

Lattice

wwwlattice-group.co.uk
www.pertemps.co.uk

Scottish Power plc

Scottish Power

www.know-us.co.uk

know-us@scottishpower.com

No. of vacancies: We will be looking to recruit 50 graduates.

Disciplines involved: We expect a good honours degree, any disciplines required vary by function. See our website for details.

Types of work offered: Business management, marketing, engineering, human resources, finance and IT.

Salary: You can expect a competitive salary based on function, qualifications and experience.

Application procedure: Online application available at company website. Alternatively talk to our recruitment team quoting reference SP19.

Scottish Power are one of the worlds top investor-owned utilities, and the UK's biggest. But there's more to us than that. Electricity, gas, water, telecoms, retail - even internet services.

WWW.CHOICESONLINE.COM

Thames Water

www.twgraduaterecruitment.com

The Graduate Recruitment Team, Clearwater Court, Vastern Road, Reading, RG1 8DB
t: 0118 373 8582

Business description:
Thames Water is the UK's largest water company and the 3rd largest water company in the world. With 43 million customers in 44 countries, we cover all aspects of water business from customer service to engineering consultancy, from drinking water to treatment of waste.

N of vacancies:
We have approximately 30-40 vacancies.

Opportunities available:
Our Graduate Development Programme is designed to improve personal skills and team building. We recruit onto Mechanical, Electrical, Civil & Chemical Engineering, Finance, Human Resources and General Business Programmes.

Application procedure:
Application forms can be obtained on the web-site or by calling 0118 373 8582 for a paper version

More information about the company, our application process and our Graduate Development Programme is available on-line at www.twgraduaterecruitment.com

Voluntary Sector

BUNAC . . . . www.bunac.org.uk

CAFOD . . . . www.cafod.org.uk
Christian Aid . . . . www.christian-aid.org.uk
Oxfam. . . . . www.oxfam.org.uk
Raleigh International Trust . . . . www.raleigh.org.uk
UNICEF . . . . www.unicef.org.uk
VSO . . . . www.vso.org.uk
Wateraid . . . . www.wateraid.org.uk
World Wide Fund for Nature (UK) . . . . www.wwf-uk.org

CATEGORIES

WEB SITES

A

B

E

P

X Y Z

www.choicesonline.com

1. Make a list of your favourite employers

2. Print out their details for your records

3. Register your interest at the click of a button

4. Subscribe to their Jobs by Email services at a single pass

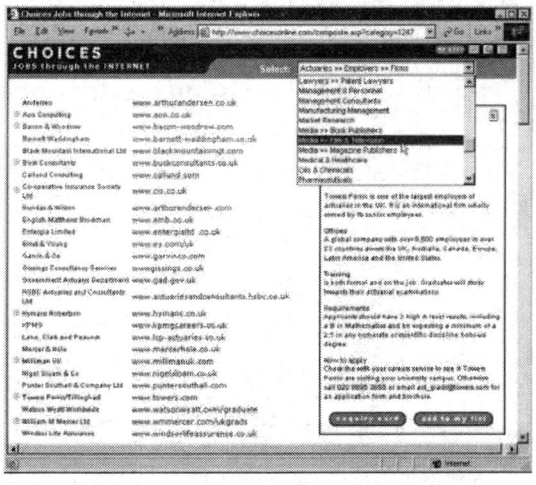

www.choicesonline.com

1. Make a list of your favourite employers

2. Print out their details for your records

3. Register your interest at the click of a button

4. Subscribe to their Jobs by Email services at a single pass

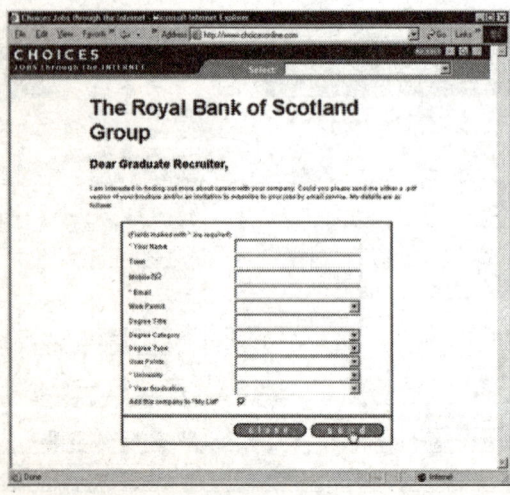